William James and John Dewey

Books by Gordon H. Clark

Readings in Ethics (1940)
Selections from Hellenistic Philosophy (1940)
A History of Philosophy (coauthor, 1941)
A Christian Philosophy of Education (1946, 1988)
A Christian View of Men and Things (1952, 1991)
What Presbyterians Believe (1956)[1]
Thales to Dewey (1957, 1989)
Dewey (1960)[2]
Religion, Reason, and Revelation (1961, 1986)
William James (1963)[2]
Karl Barth's Theological Method (1963)
The Philosophy of Science and Belief in God (1964, 1987)
What Do Presbyterians Believe? (1965, 1985)
Peter Speaks Today (1967)[3]
The Philosophy of Gordon H. Clark (1968)
Biblical Predestination (1969)[4]
Historiography: Secular and Religious (1971, 1994)
II Peter (1972)[3]
The Johannine Logos (1972, 1989)
Three Types of Religious Philosophy (1973, 1989)
First Corinthians (1975, 1991)
Colossians (1979, 1989)
Predestination in the Old Testament (1979)[4]
First and Second Peter (1980)
Language and Theology (1980, 1993)
First John (1980, 1992)
God's Hammer: The Bible and Its Critics (1982, 1987)
Behaviorism and Christianity (1982)
Faith and Saving Faith (1983, 1990)
In Defense of Theology (1984)
The Pastoral Epistles (1984)
The Biblical Doctrine of Man (1984, 1992)
The Trinity (1985, 1990)
Logic (1985, 1988)
Ephesians (1985)
Clark Speaks From the Grave (1986)
Logical Criticisms of Textual Criticism (1986, 1990)
First and Second Thessalonians (1986)
Predestination (1987)
The Atonement (1987)
The Incarnation (1988)
Today's Evangelism: Counterfeit or Genuine? (1990)
Essays on Ethics and Politics (1992)
Sanctification (1992)
New Heavens, New Earth (1993)
The Holy Spirit (1993)
An Introduction to Christian Philosophy (1993)
Lord God of Truth (1994)
William James and John Dewey (1995)

---

[1]Revised as *What Do Presbyterians Believe?* in 1965.
[2]Combined in 1995 as William James and John Dewey
[3]Combined as *First and Second Peter* (1980) and revised as *New Heavens, New Earth* (1993).
[4]Combined as *Predestination* (1987)

William James and John Dewey

Gordon H. Clark

The Trinity Foundation
Hobbs, New Mexico

Published by The Trinity Foundation
Post Office Box 1666
Hobbs, New Mexico 88240
ISBN: 0-940931-43-5

Contents

Foreword

In the early twentieth century the American philosophical world belonged to William James and John Dewey. James—psychologist and philosopher—was the older of the two; Dewey—also a psychologist and philosopher—was by far the more prolific.

James was the grandson of William James, a Calvinist businessman who emigrated from Ireland to the United States in 1798. He made his fortune by investing in the Erie Canal, and his children were saved the chore of earning their livings. His son, Henry James the elder, rejected his father's Calvinism while he was a student at Princeton Theological Seminary and became a disciple of Emanuel Swedenborg. The elder Henry James reared two famous sons, William the philosopher and Henry the novelist.

William James received his M.D. from Harvard Medical School in 1869 but never practiced medicine. He read the idealist philosopher Charles Renouvier and became convinced of free will. James wrote: "My first act of free will shall be to believe in free will."

After publishing *The Principles of Psychology* in 1890, James turned his attention away from psychology, that "nasty little subject," and toward an analysis of religious experience. Influenced by his Swedenborgian father, James had long been interested in religious experiences. He had helped organize the American Society for Psychical Research in 1884, and he published *The Varieties of Religious Experience* in 1902. Other volumes in philosophy soon followed: *Pragmatism, A New Name for Old Ways of Thinking* (1907), *A Pluralistic Universe* (1909), *The Meaning of Truth* (1909), and posthumously, *Some Problems in Philosophy* (1911) and *Essays in Radical Empiricism* (1912).

By the end of his life, reports one scholar, James was a legendary figure—a new prophet—and he was generally regarded as the chief representative of American philosophy.

James' younger contemporary, John Dewey, had published several books before James died, but his greatest influence did not begin until 1904 when he left the University of Chicago for Columbia University in New York. Through the auspices of Columbia Teachers College, which trained teachers from all over the world, Dewey spread his philosophical and educational ideas far and wide. Perhaps no other single person has had as much influence on American education as John Dewey. His bibliography runs for 150 pages—an overwhelming mass of material.

A socialist, Dewey was a trustee of Hull House in Chicago, one of the founders and the first president of the American Association of University Professors, a charter member of the first teachers union in New York City, a founder of the New School for Social Research, and an official of the American Civil Liberties Union and the League for Industrial Democracy.

It is not, however, either the political or educational ideas of James and Dewey that are the focus of this book; they are mentioned only in passing. Rather, the focus is on their underlying philosophies, without which their social views would be incomplete. Both men were non—perhaps more accurately—anti-Christian. In metaphysics they were atheists; in epistemology, pragmatic empiricists. Clark, the most eminent Christian philosopher of the twentieth century, subjects their arguments and conclusions to a rigorous and penetrating analysis, and when he is finished, there is little left of these icons of pragmatic American philosophy. There is no better analysis, from a Christian perspective, of the philosophies of William James and John Dewey than the book you hold in your hands.

John W. Robbins
December 1994

WILLIAM JAMES
1842–1910

1

INTRODUCTION

Perhaps the first thing to be said about William James—seeing that popular opinion regards all philosophical writing as dull and dreary—is that his style is intensely interesting. Far removed from the desiccated technique of Aristotle and Kant, his writings combine the literary flair of Plato with the pungency of New England. On his pages a squirrel runs around a tree, and a hunter goes around the tree, too, but does the hunter go around the squirrel? There is a train-load of passengers robbed by a few bandits; there is also the lodger whose bank account is inversely proportional to his honesty. Beyond all question, William James is interesting. His *Varieties of Religious Experience* sustains attention better than Sherlock Holmes, and one should read the two volumes of his personal letters as well as his philosophical books.

Now, the plan of this monograph is threefold. First and indispensable is a large amount of exposition. Students, of course, must have some idea of what James taught. Since *A Pluralistic Universe* and *Pragmatism* are his most characteristic books, they will furnish most of the material. The exposition will not only quote them frequently, but even where quotation marks do not appear, much of the phraseology is taken from the text. Second, the monograph will contain a certain amount of parenthetical reflection on special points. Some criticism, while not sufficiently important to be put in the conclusion, is still worth a passing mention. Then, third, the entire monograph, written from a definite point of view—as all philosophic writing must be—is designed to help the defense and development of Christian theism. Most of this help may be negative: either simply adverse criticism of James's position or the utilization of his arguments against other non-Christian philosophies. Yet possibly there could emerge something more positive also.

The first paragraph mentioned James's interesting style. This is, however, a mixed blessing. Perchance James is too popular. His illustrations run away with themselves. The absence of Aristotelian and Kantian desiccation may be an absence of exactitude and clarity. But if ambiguity contaminates his proposals, his proposals are unmistakable. For this reason it is best to begin with those points in previous philosophy which excited his reaction.

2

The Philosophic Background

The nineteenth century was characterized by two philosophic trends, both of which displeased James. The first was the absolute idealism of Hegel and his right-wing followers. This type of thought he scotches as "the serpent of rationalism." His argument will be detailed below. Inasmuch as Christianity exhibits still worse characteristics, he denounces theism too, both in his personal letters and in his formal publications.

For example, in one of his letters, written to Henry W. Rankin from Edinburgh on June 16, 1901, he says,

> I believe myself to be (probably) permanently incapable of believing the Christian scheme of vicarious salvation. . . . The mother sea and fountain head of all religions lie in the mystical experiences of the individual, taking the word mystical in a very wide sense. All theologies and all ecclesiasticisms are secondary growths superimposed; and the experiences make such flexible combinations with the intellectual prepossessions of their subjects, that one may almost say that they have no proper *intellectual* deliverance of their own, but belong to a region deeper, and more vital and practical, than that which the intellect exhibits.

Or, again (to James Henry Leuba, April 17, 1904),

> I have no living sense of commerce with a God . . . yet there is something in me which makes response when I hear utterances made from that lead by others. . . . I am sure it is not old theistic habits and prejudices of infancy. They are Christian; and I have grown so out of Christianity that entanglement therewith on the

> part of a mystical utterance has to be abstracted from and overcome, before I can listen.

Along with Hegelianism, the second characteristic of the nineteenth century displeasing to James was mechanistic scientism. Although these two seem at first sight to be deadly enemies—mind versus matter, freedom versus necessity, apriorism versus experimentation—they nonetheless agree that the world is rational. They are both forms of monism. The one says that all is spirit; the other holds that atoms alone are real. One way or the other, either in the form of scientific law or in the form of logical categories, these two philosophies assume that there is an antecedent universal order which the philosopher must discover.

In opposition to all this, James found congenial inspiration in the American philosopher, Charles Sanders Peirce (1839–1914), and in the French thinkers, Renouvier and Boutroux. From them he derived—or perhaps one should rather say, in them he found support for—his pluralism, chance, disorder, and a "blooming, buzzing confusion." Boutroux had denied logical and mathematical necessity. Logic and mathematics might have been different from what they are. The world is not mechanically determined, but is contingent, without causal relations between events.

Renouvier, to whom James acknowledged a great debt, accepted a sort of pluralism, stressed empiricism, and favored chance and free will. Deeply impressed by the differences of every kind in nature, discarding the monstrous idols of metaphysics—infinity, substance, and necessity—he sought, not a vague unity, but a plurality of concrete facts. Bits of experience occur like pieces of a jigsaw puzzle, and we must fit them together as best we can. Since we do not see the picture first, we can arrange the pieces only in some probable order. Though our emotions should not be allowed to control our reason, still we must not permit our reason to suppress our moral and religious needs. These are as much elements of experience as sensations are. Monism and pantheism, however, cannot satisfy these needs. No pantheism can withstand the notions of time, discontinuity, and freedom. Theism is equally bad, for *I Am That I*

Am is merely a religious form of the Absolute. Polytheism is far better.

Charles Sanders Peirce, of whom no adequate account can be given here, asserted that there is real chance in the universe: not that everything is as disorderly and haphazard as it could possibly be, but that, at the very least, it is not totally determined and harmonious. A few quotations will be worth the space they take up: "There is room for doubt whether the fundamental laws of mechanics hold good for single atoms, and it seems quite likely that they are capable of motion in more than three dimensions" (*Philosophical Writings of Peirce,* ed. by Justus Buchler, 318).

In *The Doctrine of Necessity Examined,* Peirce asserts that mechanism has been made a postulate of science; but "to postulate a proposition is no more than to hope it is true" (326).

> I do not believe that anybody . . . can maintain that the precise and universal conformity of facts to law is clearly proved, or even rendered particularly probable, by any observations hitherto made (331).
>
> The mechanical philosopher leaves the whole specification [the particular details] of the world utterly unaccounted for, which is pretty nearly as bad as to baldly attribute it to chance. I attribute it altogether to chance, it is true, but to chance in the form of spontaneity which is to some degree regular (337).
>
> Mechanical law, which the scientific infallibilist tells us is the only agency of nature, can never produce diversification. . . . So, if observed facts point to real growth they point to another agency, to spontaneity for which infallibilism provides no pigeonhole (357).

These anticipations therefore instruct us, as we proceed into the main exposition of James's views, to watch for the replacement of monism by pluralism; of absolute logic by pragmatic experience; and of rigid law by chance, free will, and a right to assert religious values. And, so far as interdependent topics can be given an order, it is in this order that they will be discussed.

3

A Pluralistic Universe

James opens his volume of this title by noting in England a growing interest in pluralism, humanism, and empiricism, and a diminishing interest in Hegelianism. This newer empiricism is indebted to T. H. Green because it was he who pointed out the crudities of the older, untenable empiricism. Green emphasized *relating* as the great intellectual activity and attacked the disconnectedness of the reigning English sensationism. Granted that Green was an Hegelian, a devout monist who disdained empiricism and identified man with intelligence as such; but in exposing "the chopped straw of psychology and of associationism," the flaws of earlier British thought, he made possible the wave of revised empiricism.

James defines his terms: "Empiricism means the habit of explaining wholes by parts, and rationalism means the habit of explaining parts by wholes" (7–8).

At this early stage it is no doubt inappropriate to judge between the merits of empiricism and rationalism thus defined. Yet exposition should be accompanied by a little reflection. Therefore, one may ask whether in general wholes can be explained in terms of their parts. For example, a circle cannot be explained in terms of its arcs because an arc is defined in terms of a circle. Or, again, a great painting, such as Rembrandt's *Night Watch,* is a whole properly without parts. Its beauty is not explained by square inches of colored canvas; on the contrary, the position of the colors is determined by the concept of the whole: so also a single chapter in a great novel. In view of these examples, it is justifiable to ask whether the world as a whole can be explained by its parts; that is, whether empiricism is a satisfactory philosophy.

James insists that no other method of explanation is open to us. The only material we have for making a picture of the whole world is supplied by its parts. We can invent no new forms of conception, applicable to the whole, which were not suggested by the parts. For this reason, James asserts, all philosophers, rationalists and monists as well as others, have conceived of the whole world after the analogy of some one of its particular features. The theists take their cue from manufacture (which by the way is not the truth), the pantheists from growth. Other philosophers picture the world as a grammatical sentence, in which case the whole must be logically prior to the parts, for letters would never have been invented without syllables to spell, nor syllables without words and sentences to utter.

This last example, like the arc and the art, seems at first sight to favor rationalism; but James insists that all analogies are taken from one or another of the world's subdivisions. While their proponents suppose them to be logically necessary, it is easily seen, says James, that they are all accidents of personal preference. Now, personal visions are sometimes very valuable, but none is the sole logically necessary view of the whole.

There are only a few basic types of vision or preference. A cynical personality prefers and chooses materialism; a sympathetic character adopts a spiritualistic philosophy. The former defines the world so as to leave man's soul as a sort of outside passenger or alien, while the latter insists that the intimate and human must surround and underlie the brutal.

Now, spiritualism divides into two species, one more intimate and monistic, the other less intimate and dualistic; the former is pantheism, the latter is theism. James's preferences here are mixed, so it seems; for while he rejects Hegelianism, he warmly favors intimacy. The great defect of theism is precisely its small degree of intimacy. A great anthropomorphic God would preserve the humanity of the universe; for, so conceived, God and man would be of the same spiritual species. Even so, this is not the same degree of intimacy found in pantheism's fusion of God and man, which makes us entitatively one with God. But what is worse is orthodoxy's rejection of anthropomorphism in favor of transcendence. God is eternally complete; by a free act he throws off the world as an extraneous substance, and man is a third substance extraneous to the world as well as to God. God and man are not of the same spiritual species; they are "*toto genere* distinct . . . they have absolutely *nothing* in common" (26).

This anticipation of Karl Barth's *Totally Other*—which in fact is not a Christian or Biblical concept at all—entails the consequences that God is not heart of our heart, but rather our magistrate whom we must mechanically obey. His commands, however strange, are our only moral duty. In the sphere of reason, truth is already established without our help. It is not as if the world came to know itself, or God came to know himself, partly through us; but truth exists *per se* and absolutely by God's grace and decree.

In view of the pluralism that James will defend, one might think he would regard dualistic theism as at least one step better than pantheistic monism. But such is his antipathy to Christianity that "it has to be confessed that this dualism and lack of intimacy has always operated as a drag on Christian thought. . . . God as intimate soul and reason of the universe has always seemed to some people a more worthy conception than God as external creator" (28). Even the illiterate natives of India find the doctrine of creation a puerility.

Of course it is true that mystics, Hindus, and absolute monists do not prefer theism and creation. James asserts that the idea of God as a creator and moral governor sounds as odd "as if it were some outlandish savage religion." But James feels this way because he was born with such a sympathetic, intimate character. He does not like to be a true individual—empiricist though he is, explaining wholes by parts—but much prefers to merge himself intimately with the universe and cease to be William James. But other people think that mysticism is confusion, that intimacy (whatever that means) is a drag on monism, and that illiterate Hindus are not to be accepted as theological oracles. Then, further, there is the general question of morality. James has already in these few pages made a number of moral pronouncements, and he will make a good many more. We must, therefore, particularly remember to examine how or whether he can establish his moral principles, or any moral principles, without recourse to a moral governor of the universe.

James's reliance on moral judgments and the meaninglessness of the term *intimacy* are both exemplified when he says, "Not to demand intimate relations with the universe, and not to wish them satisfactory, should be accounted signs of something wrong." But how can anyone be intimate with the universe, or any part of it, except persons and perhaps a pet dog? To talk of being intimate with a cement driveway or with Pike's Peak is to use words without meaning.

However, James rather agrees with the monists that the universe is personal. Human substance is identified with divine substance. But—whereas Absolutism thinks that this substance becomes divine only in the form of totality, the *all*-form—James prefers the pluralistic view that there may be no *all*-form at all, that substance may never get totally collected, and that the *each*-form is logically as acceptable and empirically as probable.

On the face of it this seems to mean, following Renouvier's polytheism, that James himself is a god. But it is still hard to think of the cement driveway as a god. If *each* part of the universe without exception is divine, does the term *divine* convey any more meaning than the term *intimate*?

Whether or not pluralism makes sense for others, James is convinced that monism itself is inconsistently pluralistic. On Hegelian principles, the world is the knowledge of the Absolute. The universe and the Absolute Mind are but two names for the same thing. But note, the Absolute produces the philosopher by thinking him. Then the philosopher thinks the universe. This latter thinking is not numerically distinct from the Absolute's own knowledge of itself; it is not a duplicate or copy, but part of it. As the Absolute takes me, I appear or exist with everything else in its field of perfect knowledge. But as I take myself, I appear without most other things in my field of relative ignorance. Now, ignorance breeds mistakes, and I suffer pain and misfortune. The Absolute, of course, knows that I am ignorant and that I suffer pain; but the Absolute does not suffer, nor can it be ignorant. Factors or experiences true of the world in its finite aspects cannot therefore be true of the Absolute, of the world as a whole. Thus, insofar as it is finite and plural, its knowledge of itself is different from its knowledge of itself as whole and infinite.

This radical discrepancy is a bar to intimacy almost as great as is found in theism. We humans are incurably finite and temporal. The ways of the eternal are not our ways; when *The Monist* in its original prospectus urged us to "imitate the all," it urged the impossible.

Monistic Idealism

James continues to base his pluralism on the vague principle of intimacy. Philosophers, unfortunately, have always been interested in cleaning up the litter with which the world is apparently filled. They have had a constant urge toward the neatness of monism. Pluralism, James admits, is a turbid, muddled, gothic sort of affair, and at first may excite only contempt. But the Absolute, and F.H. Bradley has made it undeniable, is foreign to us.

> It is neither intelligence nor will, neither a self nor a collection of selves, neither truthful, good, nor beautiful. . . . It is, in short, a metaphysical monster. . . . As absolute . . . the world repels our sympathy because it has no history. . . . [It] neither acts, nor suffers, nor loves, nor hates; it has no needs, desires, or aspirations. . . . [But] I am finite once for all, and all the categories of my sympathy are knit up with the finite world. . . . If we were *readers* only of the cosmic novel, things would be different; we should then share the author's point of view and recognize villains to be as essential as heroes in the plot. But we are not the readers but the very personages of the world drama (47–49).

Each of us is for himself the hero, and the villains are the men who oppose us.

> The world that each of us feels most intimately at home with is that of beings with histories that play into our history. . . . It is surely a merit in a philosophy to make the very life we lead seem real and earnest. Pluralism, in exorcising the Absolute, exorcises the great derealizer of the only life we are at home in (49).

If this defense of pluralism seems too emotional, James balances it against the equally emotional phrases of the absolutists:

> "I yielded myself to the perfect whole," writes Emerson; and where can you find a more mind-dilating object? When you accept the beatific vision of what *is,* in contrast with what *goes on,* you feel as if you had fulfilled an intellectual duty (51).

Having thus balanced emotional phrases of admiration, James then undertakes technically to refute the argument that the Absolute is the presupposition of all knowing and thinking. First, James states Lotze's argument: If many distinct beings, *a, b, c,* etc., exist independently of each other, then *a* cannot act on *b*. To act is to exert an influence. Does the influence detach itself from *a* and find *b*? If so, how does the detached influence act on *b*? By another influence, perhaps? But if in fact *b* is acted upon, then *b* must already have had the capacity to receive the action; that is, *b*'s nature was somehow fitted to *a*'s nature in advance. Therefore *a* and *b* are not distinct and independent beings.

James replies that this is a purely verbal argument. The words *independent* and *distinct,* taken abstractly, suggest only disconnection; and from disconnection mutual influence cannot be deduced. Lotze then changes the words; he calls *a* and *b* interdependent, united, one; and behold, they can now interact.

James has a point in that the word *interaction,* or even the recognition of interdependence, does not explain the particular action of a particular *a* on an equally particular *b*. But it is not so clear that Lotze's argument was purely verbal, for he was not attempting to explain a particular interaction in its particularity; he was attempting to show that any interaction presupposes a prior relationship of some sort, a prior adjustment of *b* to *a*. James is hardly justified in rejecting monism simply because its general argument does not explain a concrete situation in its concreteness. He complains that absolutists always think in extremes and never see degrees of independence, degrees of chance, and degrees of free will. (What is a degree of free will?) He insists that there are some connections between things; but

> Absolutism, on its side, seems to hold that "some" is a category ruinously infected with self-contradictoriness, and that the only categories inwardly consistent and therefore pertinent to reality are "all" and "none."

It is possible, however, that James has fallen into a little confusion here. In his reference to all and none, he seems to say that every finite object must, according to Absolutism, be related to every other finite object in every conceivable way. Two must be both greater than and less than three. An object cannot have just some relation without having all relations. But assuredly this is not the position of Absolutism. Absolutism, and theism, too, hold that everything must be related to everything else in some way; there are no two things utterly independent, though in spite of Lotze, they may nonetheless be distinct.

Now, James, on this page, seems to say that everything is related somehow to everything else. At least his words are, "As if I must necessarily be an uncontrolled monomanic insanely denying any connection whatever." This was his ejaculation in face of the absolutist's insistence, "But surely, *surely* there must be *some* connection among things!" The absolutist meant some connection among all things. Therefore when James refuses to be an uncontrolled monomanic, he must be understood to assert some relationship among all things. Otherwise his reply does not squarely oppose the absolutist. But we shall see that on other pages James explicitly denies a relationship among all things. He asserts that some things are utterly unrelated to and independent of some other things. But this argument here neither establishes pluralism nor disproves monism.

Hegel and His Method

Theism seems always to embarrass James. Shall he prefer it to Absolutism because of its dualism, or shall he prefer Absolutism because of its greater degree of intimacy? Undoubtedly intimacy wins out, and pluralism takes second place. But in any case James is sure that Absolutism and theism are not the same philosophy. Only thoroughgoing monists or pantheists have an Absolute. The God of Christianity is but one member of a pluralistic system. "I can hardly conceive of anything more different from the Absolute," says James, "than the God, say, of David or of Isaiah. That God is an essentially finite being *in* the cosmos, not with the cosmos in him" (111).

One may thank James for seeing so clearly what the liberal theologians of the nineteenth century perceived dimly, if at all. Christianity is not Hegelianism. But whatever plausibility James wishes to claim for Pluralism, it cannot be borrowed from any popular acceptance of Christianity. His assertion that the God of Christianity is but one member of a pluralistic system is not unambiguously true. While persons are not parts of God, as they are parts of the Absolute (and in this sense Christianity may be termed a pluralism) yet divine Providence unifies the world in a way that James is unwilling to accept. And in any case James is quite mistaken when he speaks of God as an essentially finite being *in* (italics his) the cosmos. Not only does James misunderstand the infinite power and the complete omniscience of God, but he also contradicts the well-known principle that "in Him we live and move and have our being." Similarly, James is equally mistaken when he adds, "He and we stand outside of each other, *just as* [italics mine] the devil, the saints, and the angels stand outside of both of us" (110). These inaccuracies should be pointed out because insofar as objections to theism and the plausibility of pluralism are based on a misstatement of Christianity, so far is James's argument weakened.

Beyond this, James relies on the problem of evil as a conclusive objection to monism, and doubtless to theism too. Pluralism, he tells us, escapes this difficulty. If there is a perfect Absolute, evil must find its source in it, for there is no other source of anything. And, no doubt, this is not very intimate; nor is it rational. Leibniz's best of all possible worlds, with a Supreme Monad which does not share its creatures' imperfections, who in their turn do not share the Creator's atoning vision of the whole, is an insoluble puzzle, both intellectually and morally.

To this objection the Absolutist has a reply that a theist cannot consistently use. Since the Absolute is the whole, the finite beings are its constituent parts. To demand that the parts be perfect is to demand that they be not parts but the Absolute. But James warns that this reply is really a pluralistic weapon: "The notion that the Absolute is made of constituents on which its being depends is the rankest empiricism." And he concludes,

> The ideally perfect whole is certainly that whole of which the parts also are perfect. . . . The Absolute is defined as the ideally perfect whole, yet most of its parts, if not all, are admittedly imperfect. Evidently the conception lacks internal consistency. . . . It creates a speculative puzzle . . . from which a pluralistic metaphysics is entirely free (124).

Pluralism escapes the problem of evil by not investigating its origin. It takes evil as an inexplicable fact and asks only how we can lessen it.

The Compounding of Consciousness

The problem of evil and questions of morality will recur in a later part of the discussion. For a little while longer, however, the case against Absolutism must be pursued by examining the relation of parts to wholes. Recall that James had defined rationalism as the tendency to explain parts by wholes and had accepted for himself the empirical procedure of explaining wholes by parts. As a caution, this monograph mentioned that arcs are ordinarily explained by circles and that an aesthetic object need not have aesthetic parts. James himself recognizes this, and it is instructive to see what he does with it.

In his earlier psychological writings, James had entertained the notion of a sort of mental chemistry. As the combination of hydrogen and oxygen produces water, so a combination of simpler mental states produces not only a more inclusive mental state but a qualitatively different one. To use his own illustration,

> We can't say that the awareness of the alphabet as such is nothing more than twenty-six awarenesses, each of a separate letter; for those are twenty-six distinct awarenesses, of single letters *without* others, while their so-called sum is one awareness, of every letter *with* its comrades. There is thus something new in the collective consciousness (188).

Since James was unwilling to admit the existence of a self or soul or other agent of combination, he treated the consciousness of the alphabet as a twenty-seventh fact, the substitute and not the sum of the twenty-six simpler consciousnesses. Again he illustrates,

> Say what you will, twelve thoughts, each of a single word, are not the self-same mental thing as one thought of the whole sentence. The higher thoughts, I insisted, are psychic units, not compounds (189).

During the years he held this view, James, in consistency, applied its principles to the Absolute; that is, thc Absolute cannot be a sum of parts. The great transcendentalist metaphor has always been a grammatical sentence. Although the sentence is composed of syllables and words, a knowledge of each does not guarantee an understanding of the whole. So, we finite beings know a word or clause, but the Absolute thinks the whole sentence. Note, too, that language did not begin with the invention of separate words, but with the desire to express complete statements. Similarly, the Absolute is the precondition of our finite thoughts. We are but its verbal fragments.

Now, James very clearly believes that with respect to sentences and "literally to such a multitude of the minor wholes of experience," this principle applies. Parenthetically, then, it may be suggested that James cannot be a thoroughgoing empiricist. In these cases at least he follows the rationalistic procedure. However, a pluralist may perhaps be allowed to accept a plurality of epistemologies. It would be too monistic to hold consistently to one only.

But though this rationalistic principle holds in many minor cases, argues James, it is of no real aid to Absolutism. When analyzed carefully, the notion that we are constituent parts of the Absolute's eternal field of consciousness raises great difficulties.

For example, if the Absolute makes us by knowing us, we cannot exist otherwise than *as* it knows us. Now, it knows each of us indivisibly from everything else, as the words of a sentence are known together when the whole sentence is understood. But we ourselves experience ourselves ignorantly and in division; we have doubts and curiosities which cannot trouble the Absolute. Therefore, in fact, we do exist otherwise than as the Absolute knows us.

Theism, James admits, does not face this objection. As distinguished from the Absolute, the God of Christianity by creating men endows them with a perseity that the Absolute cannot give. Theism might suppose that God is a mental agent who unifies in one vision the contents of our several minds. But pantheistic idealism with its insistence that we are literally *parts* of God, or, rather, of the Absolute, can allow man to exist only *as* the Absolute experiences him.

Further reflection, however, led James to modify these earlier psychology-inspired objections to Absolutism. He was perplexed, resentful, and envious because the Absolutists brushed aside these objections as if they were trivial. Since the objections weighed so heavily with James—they seemed to be logically compelling—the

Absolutists should at least have tried to face them instead of ignoring them. To James it seemed that the Absolutists used a type of intellectualist logic to establish their position and then disregarded the same logic when it was used to attack them.

Absolutism faces a dilemma. If all existence is mental, as they assert, then mental states are as they appear. No one pretends that pain as such only appears like pain, but in itself is different. But if this is so, the higher and lower levels in the universe cannot be entitatively identical, as they also assert.

Or, on the other hand, the Absolutists might retain the principle that mental existence is as it appears and posit a distinct agent of unification to do the work of an all-knower, just as our respective souls or selves are supposed in common opinion to do the work of partial knowers. Yet, in spite of lip service to Kant's transcendental unity of apperception (as if it were a combining agent), monism is unfriendly to souls or agents and speaks of the Absolute as constituted by the finite experiences themselves. It is the alphabet, but we are the letters: not indeed as if the alphabet were something additional to the letters, but rather as if it were only another name for the letters themselves. The *all*-form no doubt differs from the *each*-form, but the contents of both are the same. However, this again contradicts the idealistic principle that a mental fact is just what it appears to be; that is, pluralism is inescapable. It is simply impossible to treat a collective experience of any grade whatsoever as logically identical with a set of distributive experiences.

Nevertheless, James is not altogether satisfied with this argument against monism. It leads him in a direction he does not care to go. If in psychology we regard each complex mental fact as a separate entity, superseding others which are erroneously called its parts but not really composed of them, then in theology we should have to replace Absolutism with theism. Such is the force of logic. But theism is so intolerable that we are now forced to question our loyalty to logic.

The vision of the Absolutists in unscrupulously allowing mental fields to compound themselves so as to make the universe more continuous cannot be a contradiction incarnate. James, pluralist though he was, wanted to be as monistic as he possibly could be. Therefore, if logic conflicts with the vision of the Absolutists, so much the worse for logic. "Logic, being the lesser thing, the static incomplete abstraction, must succumb to reality, not reality to logic" (907). Therefore, the Absolutists were justified in ignoring the intellectualistic objections to their theory.

James thus found himself in an impasse, a dilemma, or, rather, a trilemma. Either he would have to abandon "psychology without a soul" (to which his whole scientific and Kantian education had committed him), in which case he would have to reintroduce spiritual agents who would do the knowing and combining of mental states;* or else he would have to confess that the problem was insoluble and either give up intellectualistic logic or admit that life

---

*James's antipathy to a unifying soul or self led him into what seems to be a thoroughgoing behaviorism. The title of the first of the *Essays in Radical Empiricism* asks, "Does Consciousness Exist?" The answer is, No. What is vaguely designated under the term *consciousness* is neither a substance, nor a way of being, but a kind of external relation. The early empiricists were wrong in understanding experience as discontinuous. Radical empiricism, on the other hand, acknowledges relations to be as real as anything else. Hence there is no need of a soul, a transcendental ego, or a self to do the unifying.

The *I think* which Descartes and Kant made to accompany all my objects, says James, is the *I breathe* which actually does accompany them. "Breath moving outwards between the glottis and the nostrils is, I am persuaded, the essence out of which philosophers have constructed the entity known to them as consciousness. That entity is fictitious" (37).

A year later (1905) James concluded another article, "La Notion de Conscience," with six theses, from which the following words are selected: "La Conscience . . . n'existe pas. Ce . . . que le mot de Conscience recouvre, c' est la susceptibilité que possèdent les parties de l'expérience d'etre rapportées ou connues. Cette susceptibilité s'explique . . . de telle sorte que les unes [parties de l'expérience] se trouvent jouer le role de choses connues, les autres celui de sujets connaissants" (232).

("Consciousness . . . does not exist. What the word *consciousness* designates is the susceptibility which parts of experience possess to be reported or known. This susceptibility is explained . . . in such a way that they [some parts of experience] turn out to play the role of things known, [and] others of knowing subjects."—*Editor*) *Note continued on next page*

is irrational. (Perhaps a reader might be excused for thinking that the last two alternatives are identical.)

Now, the first possibility—the admission of souls or spiritual agents—is barren:

> You can see no deeper into the fact that a hundred sensations get compounded or known together by thinking that a "soul" does the compounding than you see into a man's living eighty years by thinking of him as an octogenarian (209–210).

So? Doubtless no more information is contained in "octogenarian" than in "eighty years old"; but both somehow seem to presuppose a man who does the living.

Someday, James admits, souls may again be accepted; but it will only be after some pragmatic significance has been attached to them.

What then? Can we give up logic and assert that human experience is fundamentally irrational? Hegel was the first non-mystical writer to abandon ordinary logic, saving a pseudo-rationality for the universe by inventing his dialectic process. Bradley retained logic and by it convicts the human universe of being irrationality incarnate. He then adds that the Absolute is relieved of this irrationality in some secret way of its own, about which we cannot even guess.

"For my own part," says James, "I have finally found myself compelled to *give up the logic,* fairly, squarely, and irrevocably" (212). Indeed, we may say, James is logically forced to abandon logic. To be sure, logic has some use in human life. But reality, life, or experience exceeds logic, overflows and surrounds it. If it sounds unpleasant to call reality irrational, at least it is non-rational;

Behaviorism as such will not be discussed in this monograph on William James. It receives its due in the monograph on Dewey. But one may briefly note in the quotation above that the susceptibility of being known is explained by the fact that some things are known and other things are knowers. This points up the circular cloudiness of "pure experience."

> and by reality here I mean reality where things *happen*, all temporal reality without exception. I myself find no good warrant for even suspecting the existence of any reality of a higher denomination than that distributed and strung along and flowing sort of reality which we finite beings swim in (213).

But if there were a higher reality, it would be still less amenable to logic.

Conclusions

In all this argument against Absolutism and for pluralism there is a religious motivation. James's studies in the *Varieties of Religious Experience* had convinced him that religious experience was real and important. But it lies beyond reason. Reason could never have anticipated that Martin Luther's new life would supervene upon his previous despair. Nor can this experience be explained either by naturalism or by theism.

It is most strange that James should have asserted, without supporting argument, that the God of Abraham and Isaiah cannot account for Luther's conversion. One can only note that ingrained hatred of Christianity leads men to make the most absurd and palpably false statements. Maybe Absolutism might find evangelical conversion a little embarrassing, but is not this what theism *is*—is not this what God does?

However, James draws the conclusion that the varieties of religious experience point to the existence of a "wider self from which saving experiences flow in." This "wider self" may in fact be a number of selves. Fechner was clearly polytheistic, and it is only because the term *polytheism* gives offence that James refuses to use it. But at any rate, the only way to escape from the dilemmas and perplexities of Absolutism is to be frankly pluralistic and to assume that the superhuman consciousness has itself an external environment and is consequently finite: finite either in knowledge, or in power, or in both at once.

This pluralism with its finite god or gods produces a curious twist that James does not seem to notice. He continues to insist:

> Thus does foreignness get banished from our world. . . . We are indeed internal parts of God and not external creations. . . . Yet because God is not the Absolute, but is himself a part when the system is conceived pluralistically, his functions can be taken as not wholly dissimilar to those of the other smaller parts . . . (318).

Now, first, can pluralism consistently maintain that we are internal parts of God? If there are many gods, of which one are we parts? And if God also is a part, as James has just said, is not a higher Absolutism the outcome?

Since James is so vigorous in his rejection of Absolutism, let us suppose that his reference to our being internal parts of God was a slip of the pen. It must be admitted, however, that there are several slips of the pen in this section. At one point he says,

> Every part, though it may not be in actual or immediate connection, is nevertheless in some possible or mediated connection with every other part however remote, through the fact that each part hangs together with its very next neighbors in inextricable interfusion (325).

But if we discount the monistic tone of these words and continue with his vigorous pluralism, then we have a polytheism or panpsychism that he does not definitely deny and even seems to approve of. Every god then, every soul and spirit—though James wants psychology without a soul—will be a part of a pluralistic system.

> Everything you can think of, however vast or inclusive, has on the pluralistic view a genuinely "external" environment. . . . Nothing includes everything . . . something always escapes. . . . However much may be collected, however much may report itself as present at any effective center of consciousness or ac-

> tion, something else is self-governed and absent and unreduced to unity (321–322).

But now, in the second place, can this construction banish that foreignness which James finds so distasteful? No doubt I can be intimate with one god or with several, but can I be intimate with every part of this pluralistic panpsychism without being myself the effective center of consciousness to which everything is present?

Furthermore, although James asserts that pluralism refuses to ask about the source of evil, it must have some source in the cosmos. Some part of the universe, some god or other, must be its origin. Can I then, assuming of course that I am as good as James thinks himself to be, be intimate and sympathetic with the evil as well as with the good? These are questions whose answers are not easily found in James's pluralism, problems swept under the rug along with logic. To the type of religion involved and to the distinction between good and evil, we shall have to return later on.

4

PRAGMATISM

In the preceding account of James's pluralism, it was seen that he opposes intellectualism and repudiates logic. Two years before the publication of *A Pluralistic Universe,* he had published *Pragmatism* in which truth and logic are amply discussed.

What Pragmatism Means

It is under this title that James asks whether a hunter goes around a squirrel, if, while he is walking around the tree, the squirrel always keeps on the opposite side of the trunk. The solution James proposed to the hunting party as it sat around the fireplace that cold winter night was simply two definitions of the term *around.* If one means to the north, east, south, and west of the squirrel, the answer is yes; but if one means in front of, on the right, to the rear of, and on the left of, the answer is no.

But instead of accepting this solution as a mere matter of scholastic definition, James draws the conclusion that the concept "around," and any concept, means its *practical* consequences. When one asks, Is the world one or many? Material or spiritual?

> the pragmatic method in such cases is to try to interpret each notion by tracing its respective practical consequences. . . . If no practical difference whatever can be traced, then the alternatives mean practically the same thing (45).

James credits Peirce with the discovery of this pragmatic principle. Asserting that all beliefs are really rules for action, Peirce held that to develop a thought's meaning we need only determine what conduct it is fitted to produce: that conduct is for us its sole significance. No matter how subtle the concept, it consists of nothing else than a possible difference in practice.*

"Our conceptions of these effects," says James, "our reactions, our sensations, the 'practical consequences,' whether immediate or remote, is then for us the whole of our conception of the object, so far as that conception has positive significance at all" (47).

From this it follows—must it not?—that the concept of a pluralistic universe is not a description of any reality independent of me. Its significance consists solely of my behavior. Similarly, whatever god there may be cannot exist as a consciousness other than mine; god is merely the things I do. Absolutism, on the other hand, is nothing else than the practical conduct of Hegel, Bradley, and their colleagues. Metaphysical concepts, therefore, are essentially actions to be judged by moral standards. Even mass, energy, length, and time must fall within the sphere of ethics. Each of these words, *God, matter, reason,* etc., must be given

> its practical cash-value. . . . It appears less as a solution, then, than as a program for more work, and particularly as an indication of the ways in which existing realities may be *changed. Theories thus become instruments, not answers to enigmas* (italics his; 53).

The ever-increasing emphasis on conduct, on changing things, on programs and instruments, shows more clearly with every chapter that pragmatism is basically a theory of morality.

James commends pragmatism with many fair words: It "turns away from abstraction and insufficiency . . . from bad *a priori* rea-

---

*John Dewey accuses James of ambiguity at this point. Briefly Dewey asks, "Does Mr. James employ the pragmatic method to discover the value in terms of consequences in life of some formula which has its logical content already fixed; or does he employ it to criticize and revise and ultimately to constitute the meaning of that formula?" Dewey himself never wavers in his acceptance of the second of these meanings.

sons [all *a priori* reasons are bad], from fixed principles and closed systems"; it turns toward "the open air and possibilities of nature, as against dogma, artificiality, and the pretence of finality in truth" (51).

In fact the concept pragmatism itself means differences in conduct. It means an enormous change in philosophical practice. It means that rationalistic professors would be frozen out of university positions (51–52), and only pragmatists appointed to Harvard.

Rationalism had supposed that the laws of science were the eternal thoughts of the Almighty, who thundered in syllogisms and reverberated in conic sections. But now, says James (and it has become much clearer since James's day), scientific laws are seen to be at best merely approximations. Furthermore, there are so many rival formulations that scientists acknowledge that none is a transcript of reality. They are only a man-made language exhibiting considerable human arbitrariness. That is,

> ideas . . . become true just insofar as they help us to get into satisfactory relation with other parts of our experience. . . . Any ideas upon which we can ride . . . linking things satisfactorily, working securely, simplifying, saving labor, is true for just so much, true in so far forth, true instrumentally (58).

Speaking of how new information and new discoveries—as the discovery of radium altered the concept of the conservation of energy—cause trouble among old ideas, James wrote,

> Purely objective truth, truth in whose establishment the function of giving human satisfaction in marrying previous parts played no role whatever, is nowhere to be found. The reasons why we call things true is the reason why they *are* true, for "to be true" *means* only to perform this marriage-function. . . . Truth independent; truth that we *find* merely; truth no longer malleable to human need; supposed to exist by rationalistically minded thinkers . . . means only the dead heart of the living tree, and its being

> there means only that truth also has its paleontology. . . . But how plastic even the oldest truths nevertheless really are has been vividly shown in our day by the transformation of logical and mathematical ideas . . . (64–65).

Consequently, too, "if theological ideas prove to have a value for concrete life, they will be true, for pragmatism, in the sense of being good for so much" (73). As was said before, God is my behavior. So is the Absolute my behavior. The Absolute means that we may take a moral holiday and not continually bear responsibility for the whole universe. "If the Absolute means this, and means no more than this, who can possibly deny the truth of it? To deny it would be to insist that men should never relax" (75).

But would an Absolutist, in need of a holiday, be able to relax if he were convinced that that Absolute is merely his relaxation? Is it not necessary to believe that the Absolute, or God, is something other than one's own behavior if one is to believe that things will turn out well?

Some Metaphysical Problems

Beyond the general statement of pragmatism, James is good enough to tell us what pragmatism means, not only with respect to the employment of college professors, but also with respect to some metaphysical problems. Two of these will be briefly considered here: substance and God.

Everybody uses the distinction between substance and attribute because it has become enshrined in the very structure of language as subject and object. Chalk, we suppose, is a substance whose attributes are white, cylindrical, friable, insoluble, and so on. Similarly, the attributes of this desk inhere in the substance wood, and our thoughts and feelings are properties of our substantial souls.

Yet all we *know* of these substances is their attributes. Apart from and in addition to white, cylindrical, and friable, we know nothing about chalk. The group of attributes itself is its sole cash-value for our actual experience. If we were cut off from the attributes, we should never suspect the existence of substance. Therefore, nominalists conclude that substance is a spurious idea, a mere name for a group of qualities. In reality, the properties do not inhere in anything; they adhere or cohere with each other. Behind the bare fact of cohesion is just nothing at all.

The only pragmatic value ever given to the notion of substance is the Roman Catholic dogma of transubstantiation. In this Romish superstition the properties of bread remain the same while the substance changes into the substance of Christ's body, so that the recipient eats grace. But admittedly no one could discover any of this by empirical observation; and beyond this, *substance* has no meaning at all.

The philosophical refutation of material substance was accomplished by Bishop Berkeley. This keen observer took the world to be just as it appears to be (white, cylindrical, and so on) without any unobservable matter underneath it. Berkeley therefore interpreted material substance pragmatically as merely the name for collections of sensory experiences.

John Locke (somewhat inconsistently) and David Hume applied the same criticism to spiritual substance. Rationalism had explained the practical continuity in our lives by the unity of soul-substance. But Locke and Hume argued there was no pragmatic difference between the continuity of consciousness itself and that continuity as inhering in a spiritual principle. Suppose, says James, repeating Locke, that God removed our consciousness and left us the soul principle:

> Should *we* be any the better for having still the soul-principle? Suppose he annexed the same consciousness to different souls, should *we*, as we realize *ourselves*, be any the worse for that fact? (90–91).

Soul therefore, concludes James, is but a name for the verifiable cohesions of our inner life.

In spite of the sharp opposition between materialists and spiritualists, he continues, matter and spirit in their traditional meanings are equivalents. It is true that materialism is castigated as crass and gross; spiritualism is refined and intellectual. But Herbert Spencer exposed this emotional evaluation by showing that a "matter" so infinitely subtile as to satisfy the needs of modern science has no trace of grossness left; conversely spirit, as traditionally viewed, is too gross to account for the exquisite tenuity of nature's facts. Both terms, therefore, are merely symbols of an unknowable reality in which their oppositions cease.

James does not stop here to criticize Spencer's unknowable reality, but goes on to insist that materialism and spiritualism are the same thing. What practical difference does either one make?

> It makes not a single jot of difference so far as the *past* of the world goes. . . . Imagine, in fact, the entire contents of the world to be once for all irrevocably given. Imagine it to end this very moment, and to have no future; and then let a theist and a materialist apply their rival explanations to its history. The theist shows how a God made it; the materialist shows, and we will suppose with equal success, how it resulted from blind physical forces. . . . The pragmatist must consequently say that the two theories, in spite of their different-sounding names, mean exactly the same thing (96–97).

But perhaps it is time to pause a moment and examine the construction of this challenge. There are a number of points to note.

First, let us assume that James is proceeding as a consistent pragmatist. Then so far as *past* history is concerned God and matter are equally unsuccessful as explanations because, by the pragmatic theory of truth, ideas are plans of *future* action whose cash-value is our own conduct.

But can James proceed as a consistent pragmatist and still make his challenge? To the extent that pragmatism can get rid of both God and matter by identifying them as our future conduct, perhaps the pragmatist will be satisfied. But this raises the second point as to whether pragmatism can explain the past at all. Possibly James can afford to be a little inconsistent and in some way or other allow ideas to be identified with past as well as with future events. This seems to be involved in that part of the argument where he reduces God, soul, and matter to "substances," and interprets substance as a mere name for the collections of qualities and events. In this case, God and matter would both be names for the past events themselves. But so also would be any other concept that James might consider better than these traditional ones. For this very reason James's concepts would be as worthless as God and matter, for they would not *explain* the past—they would *be* the past. On the pragmatic principles, therefore, no explanation at all can be given.

In the third place, it is now clear that James cannot construct his challenge on a strictly pragmatic basis. It must be taken as an *ad hominem* argument, for its terms make sense only upon an intellectualistic interpretation of the terms *matter* and *God*. But as an *ad hominem* argument, the challenge is poor because his opponents will not allow James to give the same meaning to the two terms. In the traditional view, *God* and *matter* have meant something quite different. *Matter* has meant inert atoms, as James himself admits (99); *God,* on the other hand, means an omnipotent intelligence. With these meanings there is a *prima facie* implausibility in supposing that they are equally successful explanations of past history. Yet the whole force of James's challenge is the twice asserted supposition of this equal success. Surely this is begging the question.

The *petitio* occurs in another form also. Only a few pages earlier, in talking about soul and substance, James had supposed that God might remove our consciousness while leaving us our soul-principle. Thus it seems that James understands or misunderstands spiritual substance as inert and unconscious. But this was not Descartes's view, nor Leibniz's, nor Berkeley's, nor Augustine's, nor the view of anyone else. In all cases the soul was defined as an active, perceiving being; and to remove the power of perception would be to destroy the soul. James's challenge therefore is constructed of contradictions.

Fourth, James also assumes in constructing this test that the world comes to an end right now and has no future. But this assumption can be made neither on pragmatic principles nor on intellectualistic principles. For James, as we have already insisted, concepts must refer to practical consequences; they are rules for action, future action. He was quoted above to the effect that God and matter are not a solution but "a program for more work, and particularly as an indication of the ways in which existing realities may be changed. *Theories thus become instruments, not answers to enigmas.*" Hence, by his own principles James cannot for himself appeal to the challenge he has constructed. No concept, not even the concept of pragmatism, would have any meaning on this supposition. Nor can the challenge of an *ad hominem* argument, since theists will not grant the world can have no future. Very pointedly the Christian theist predicts a future judgment.

It is in such a passage as this that John Dewey can find justification for his charge that James inconsistently oscillates between pragmatism and intellectualism. Sometimes James attaches an intellectualistic content to the concept God and desires it tested in experience, but at other times he argues that every concept is precisely its future effects in human behavior. Only by combining these incompatible views can he construct this puzzling, this confused, this futile challenge.

Of course, James expects a future too; and it is in connection with the future that he tries to defend some sort of a belief in God. Strange as it may seem, James argues that while matter could do everything that God could do in the past, matter cannot do what God can do in the future. "Theism and materialism, so indifferent when taken retrospectively, point, when we take them prospectively, to wholly different outlooks of experience" (103). The concept of matter points to the death of the cosmos:

> The energies of our system will decay, the glory of the sun will be dimmed. . . . Man will go down into the pit, and all his thoughts will perish. . . . The notion of God; on the other hand, . . . guarantees an ideal order that shall be permanently preserved (104–106).

The choice between these views is a moral choice. Superior minds are seriously concerned about an ideal order; materialism appeals only to shallow men. Religion incites our more strenuous moments and justifies our trust and joy. Similarly, free will is a general cosmological theory of promise; it is a religious doctrine of relief. Determinism is the absence of promise and hope. "Other than this practical significance, the words *God, free will, design,* etc. have none" (121). Define them intellectually and you stare stupidly at a pretentious sham. Pragmatism alone can give them a positive meaning.

But just one question—the same question over again: If God and free will have nothing but a pragmatic significance; if, as he repeats in the opening of the succeeding chapter, "design, free-will, the absolute mind, spirit instead of matter, have for their sole meaning a better promise as to this world's outcome" (127); if, that is, God has only the pragmatic significance of being my subjective hope, and not a transcendent, omnipotent Being intellectually defined, in what sense can "God" guarantee the preservation of an ideal order after the death of the solar system? Pragmatism, therefore, will not do what James wants done; it won't work; therefore, it is false.

Pragmatism and Common Sense

Once again James contrasts the hypothesis that the unity of the universe is found in an omniscient knower with the opposite hypothesis that the widest field of knowledge still contains some ignorance. From the fact that these are logical alternates, he immediately concludes that the second may be legitimately accepted because "we are bound to treat it as respectfully as noetic monism until the facts shall have tipped the beam; [therefore] our pragmatism, though originally nothing but a method, has forced us to be friendly to the pluralistic view" (166). Evidently James does not require much force. One must, however, grant James that our knowledge is incomplete and examine his account of how it grows.

First of all, our knowledge grows unevenly. We accept one new idea, drop one old idea, while all the rest are altered hardly at all. The change continues, but it continues very slowly. "It follows that very ancient modes of thought may have survived through all the later changes in men's opinion" (169). This residuum is what we call common sense; that is to say,

> our fundamental ways of thinking about things are discoveries of exceedingly remote ancestors, which have been able to preserve themselves throughout the experience of all subsequent time. . . . Were we lobsters or bees [we would have developed other, non-human categories]. It might be too (we cannot dogmatically deny this) that such categories, unimaginable by us today, would have proved on the whole as serviceable for handling our experiences mentally as those which we actually use (171).

That James's description fits the development and replacement of most if not all scientific concepts is undeniable. Force, mass, energy, magnetic fields, and chemical valence—so different from the concepts of Aristotle's *Physics* Book VII and James's own psychological concepts of habit and consciousness—were invented only in the recent past and have already undergone considerable modification. But is James's description applicable to all concepts? Is it enough to assert without argument that space and time, far from being Kantian intuitions, "are constructions as patently artificial as any that science can show" (178)? If this were so, if alternate concepts unimaginable by us today could have been as serviceable as space and time, then our remote ancestors would have to have had experiences outside of space and time. This indeed is too unimaginable to discuss or even to suggest.

Or, further, shall we allow James to rely on assertions such as: these concepts "*may have* been successfully discovered by prehistoric geniuses," and *"may have* spread until all language rested on them" (182–183); and from these fragile suppositions to conclude that the concepts of implication and contradiction might have been or still may be replaced with a different but now unimaginable logic? If this were possible, if the laws of logic were artificial constructs, then a philosopher could accept both monism and pluralism, both rationalism and empiricism; and every implication would be both valid and invalid at the same time.

Pragmatism's Conception of Truth

James is greatly perturbed because the rationalists have so ferociously attacked F. C. S. Schiller's and John Dewey's view of truth and have "so abominably misunderstood" it. He therefore desires to make "a clear and simple statement" of it (197).

First of all, James points out the difficulty in holding that truth is a copy of reality as a photograph is a reproduction of whatever was its object. Such an identification of truth with memory images has indeed been made in the history of philosophy, but a reference to Descartes, Hegel, and Brand Blanshard shows that the fortunes of intellectualism are not dependent on this theory. James himself admits, "some idealists seem to say that they [our ideas] are true whenever they are what God means that we ought to think about that object. . . . But the great assumption of the intellectualists," he continues, "is that truth means essentially an inert static relation" (199–200). If he had said that truth for intellectualism is a *stable* and *dependable* relation, the connotation and suggestion would have been different.

Since truth, for intellectualism, is immutable, possession of the truth, or knowledge, fulfills one's

> thinking destiny . . . and nothing more need follow on that climax of your rational destiny. . . . Pragmatism, on the other hand, asks . . . "Grant an idea or belief to be true," it says, "what concrete difference will its being true make in anyone's actual life?. . . .

> What experiences will be different from those which would obtain if the belief were false?" (200).

By so phrasing the question, James insinuates that an intellectualistic truth cannot have practical consequences, and that such attention to consequences is the prerogative solely of pragmatism.

In this, James is very much mistaken. Let the intellectualistic and immutable idea of God be a Spirit: infinite and eternal and unchangeable in his being, wisdom, power, holiness, justice, goodness, and truth. Now, if such a Spirit actually exists; that is, if this idea refers to a true reality, hundreds of practical conclusions follow. And if no such Spirit exists, then there follow hundreds of quite different practical conclusions. James therefore fails in his attempt to convict intellectualism of having no relation to conduct.

On the contrary, one wishes to learn what practical applications pragmatism can have on its theory of truth.

> The truth of an idea is not a stagnant property inherent in it. Truth *happens* to an idea. It *becomes* true, is *made* true by events. Its verity *is* in fact an event, a process: the process namely of its verifying itself, its veri-*fication*. Its validity is the process of its valid-*ation* (201).

If, now, James permits himself to call an intellectualistic idea "stagnant," cannot we with more reason interpret the preceding as an assertion that verification is a process of making false ideas true? They are not true to begin with; they must *become* true. Ergo, they start out as false. Thus pragmatism is the attempt to make the worse appear the better argument.

The process of verification, however, is not too clearly explained. One would like to know how a false idea, or at any rate an idea that is not true, is made true. James speaks of verification as a series of events or experiences which lead us into or toward other experiences so that the transitions from point to point are progressive, harmonious, and satisfactory. This statement is extremely vague, and James tries to clarify it by an example:

> If I am lost in the woods and starved, and find what looks like a cow path, it is of the utmost importance that I should think of a human habitation at the end of it, for if I do so and follow it, I save myself (203).

This example, unfortunately, does not explain how a false cow path can become a true cow path, or how the wrong direction of any path can become the right direction. Following a cow path and coming to a house might show that my idea or guess had been true all the time, but nothing James has said explains how something becomes true that previously was not. Nor, to repeat, has James succeeded in divesting antecedent, intellectualistic truth of practical importance.

Now, James does indeed protest that the making of truth is no happy-go-lucky affair. Truth is what works; but between the exigencies of sensory reality and the necessary consistency of correct thought, "the squeeze is so tight that there is little loose play for any hypothesis. Our theories are wedged and controlled as nothing else is." Yet he continues to insist: "Truth is *made* just as health, wealth, and strength are made" (217–218). As a sick man is made well, so a false idea is made true.

How, then, can James explain the rationalistic objection? Is it not quite plausible that the cow path antecedently leads (or does not lead) to a house, and that we simply discover and not make it so? James, in fact, states the objection vigorously enough: "These [verification processes] are merely signs of its being [true], merely our lame ways of ascertaining after the fact, which of our ideas already has possessed the wondrous quality" (219).

For an answer, James refers to the great number of our ideas which we take as true even though we have not directly verified them. For example, the specific gravity of gold has been verified a finite number of times, and because of these verifications we suppose that present and future instances of gold will have the same density. If we should verify a new instance, we would "discover" that it is the same as the old instances. Similarly, no doubt many individuals have verified the idea that cow paths lead to a house.

> The quality of truth, obtaining *ante rem,* pragmatically means, then, the fact that in such a world innumerable ideas work better by their indirect or possible than by their direct and actual verification. Truth *ante rem* means only verifiability (220).

This attempt, however, to push back the present difficulty to a past instance does not remove the difficulty. It still attaches to the past instance. Take some early experimenter with cow paths before several instances had been verified. The man is lost, and he sees a linear barrenness of vegetation; he then entertains the idea that this is a path and that walking toward the right rather than to the left will bring him to a house, a tent, or an inhabited cave. Does walking on this path make it go in the right direction? Does the walking make the habitation he hopes for? The problem seems no different a thousand years ago from what it is today. Our success in any instance depends on the house's being there already. Of course, our success in avoiding starvation depends on our walking also. But the truth of the assertion that a house is there depends, not on our walking, but on some antecedent builder. We certainly do not make it by walking, even in the right direction.

Admittedly James delivers telling blows against some rationalists' assertions. A. E. Taylor's definition of truth as the system of propositions which have an unconditional claim to be recognized as valid is circular at best. But when James seizes upon the idea of an unconditional claim, and denounces it, he misses the point. True enough, a concrete situation does not enforce the claim of irrelevant truth: If you ask me what time it is and I reply that I live at 95 Irving Street, my answer may be true, but there is no unconditional duty that I should thus reply to your question (232). James even says that a false address would be as much to the purpose. But does not this miss the point? The irrelevance of the answer to this specific question does not erase the difference between a true and a false address. If in a concrete sense there is no duty to give the correct address, at least there is a duty—an unconditional claim—not to give the false one.

James ridicules the notion of a reality calling on us to "agree" with it simply because its claim is "unconditional." But if there is any reality, can James advise us to disregard it? If so, I fear that his pragmatism will lose whatever plausibility it may have.

But maybe there is no reality. Of course James says there is; but he considers it malleable, almost infinitely malleable. The sensory core of reality is forced upon us, coming we know not whence. Yet we choose some sensations and ignore others. What this core may be independently of our manipulation is hard to say. "We may glimpse it, but we never grasp it. What we grasp is always some substitute for it which previous human thinking has peptonized and cooked for our consumption" (242–249).

To illustrate, James prints a six-pointed star. We can treat it, he says, as a star, or as two intertwined equilateral triangles, or as a hexagon with legs, or as six little triangles connected by their tips. Similarly, a certain constellation in the north can with equal right be called the Dipper, the Great Bear, or Charles' Wain. What we call things "seems quite arbitrary, for we carve out everything, just as we carve out constellations, to suit our human purposes" (253).

Now, no doubt the name of a constellation is quite arbitrary; and in a purely semantic sense *triangle* and *circle* are arbitrary, for *three* might have meant four and *straight* might have been applied to curves. But we cannot arbitrarily carve a circle out of the lines of intertwined equilateral triangles. Straight lines are not quite that malleable. They are somewhat fixed in a rationalistic sort of way.

At this point James returns to the antithesis of monism and pluralism, "On the pragmatist side," he says,

> we have only one edition of the universe, unfinished, growing in all sorts of places, especially in the places where thinking beings are at work. On the rationalistic side we have a universe in many editions, one real one, the infinite folio, or *edition de luxe,* eternally complete; and then the various finite editions, full of false readings, distorted and mutilated each in its own way (259).

Is it not strange that here James allies pragmatism with monism, and rationalism with pluralism? He did not have to do it this way, for rather evidently it is rationalism that has one real universe and pragmatism as many universes as there are people to make them.

It is precisely in this connection that James attributes the choice between these views to "a temperamental difference" among men.

> The rationalist mind, radically taken, is of a doctrinaire and authoritative complexion. . . . A radical pragmatist, on the other hand, is a happy-go-lucky anarchistic sort of creature. . . . The idea of this loose universe affects your typical rationalists in much the same ways as "freedom of the press" might affect a veteran official in the Russian bureau of censorship. . . . It appears as backboneless and devoid of principle as "opportunism" in politics appears to an old-fashioned French legitimist, or to a fanatical believer in the divine right of the people. . . . To rationalists this [flux of finite experiences] described a tramp and vagrant world, adrift in space, with neither elephant nor tortoise to plant the sole of its foot upon (259–261).

And James continues to contrast the "tender-minded" rationalists who feel the need of an immutable ground to support the flux with the tough-minded empiricists whose alpha and omega are facts.

Yet James is not quite willing to give unqualified approval to the tough-minded empiricists:

> Either hypothesis is legitimate in pragmatist eyes, for either has its uses. . . . Abstractly . . . the notion of the absolute world is indispensable. Concretely taken, it is also indispensable, at least to certain minds, for it determines them religiously. . . . We cannot therefore methodologically join the tough minds in their rejection of the whole notion of a world beyond our finite experience. One misunderstanding of pragmatism is to identify it with positivistic tough-mindedness. . . . I have all along been offering it [pragmatism] expressly as a mediator between tough-mindedness and tender-mindedness. If the notion of a world *ante rem* . . . can be shown to have any consequences whatever for

> our life, it has a meaning. If the meaning works, it will have *some* truth that ought to be held to through all possible reformulations, for pragmatism. The absolutistic hypothesis, that perfection is eternal, aboriginal, and most real, has a perfectly definite meaning, and it works religiously (266–270).

Pragmatism and Religion

The use of the Absolute in religion is proved by the whole course of religious history. The eternal arms are then beneath. The human situation is taken in the mystical way of pure cosmic emotion. The glories and the grandeurs are ours absolutely, despite present appearances. This is the way of quietism, of indifferentism, derided by its enemies as spiritual opium; "yet pragmatism must respect this way, for it has massive historic vindication" (276).

But pragmatism sees another way to be respected also. The glories, instead of being already certain in the past, are goals to be achieved by conquering present appearances; the unity, instead of being behind us as a necessary principle, is a possible empirical unification, a *terminus ad quem.* Intellectualism places its religious values *ante rem;* pragmatism places them *in rebus.* In the former, one lies back; in the latter, one pushes forward.

More explicitly, absolute religion makes all good things certain and all bad things impossible. Comparing this with pragmatism, one sees that "the great religious difference lies between the men who insist that the world *must and shall be,* and those who are contented with believing that the world *may be,* saved.

To say that the salvation of the world is possible means that some of the conditions of the world's deliverance actually exist. The more such, and the fewer opposing conditions, the better. Now, anyone who pretends to be indifferent and neutral with respect to the world's salvation is a fool and a shame. All of us wish to minimize the insecurity of the universe. Nonetheless, there are some

> unhappy men who think the salvation of the world is impossible. Theirs is the doctrine of pessimism. Optimism in turn would be the doctrine that thinks the world's salvation inevitable.
>
> Midway between the two there stands what may be called the doctrine of meliorism (285).

In this view salvation is neither necessary nor impossible. Salvation is a possibility, which becomes more and more of a probability as its actual conditions become more numerous.

What is it that increases the number of these desirable conditions? We do! Our acts—where we make ourselves and where we grow—are the actual turning places and growing places which they seem to be, not of ourselves only, but of the world. It is in our actions that we see fact in the making.

Irrational?

> Suppose that the world's author put the case to you before creation, saying: "I am going to make a world not certain to be saved, a world the perfection of which shall be conditional merely, the condition being that each several agent does its own level best. I offer you the chance of taking part in such a world. Its safety, you see, is unwarranted. It is a real adventure, with real danger, yet it may win through. It is a social scheme of co-operative work genuinely to be done. Will you join the procession? Will you trust yourself and trust the other agents enough to face the risk?"
>
> Should you in all seriousness, if participation in such a world were proposed to you, feel bound to reject it as not safe enough? Would you say that, rather than be a part and parcel of so fundamentally pluralistic and irrational a universe, you preferred to relapse into the slumber of nonentity from which you had been momentarily aroused by the tempter's voice?
>
> Of course if you are normally constituted, you would do nothing of the sort. There is a healthy-minded buoyancy in most of us which such a universe would exactly fit. We would therefore accept the offer—*"Top! und schlag auf schlag!"* It would

> be just like the world we practically live in; and loyalty to our old nurse Nature would forbid us to say no. The world proposed would seem "rational" to us in the most living way (290–291).

Of course, James admits, there are some morbid souls who would not agree. Nirvana means safety and this appeals to the Hindu and the Buddhist, for they are simply afraid, afraid of life.

> There can be no doubt that when men are reduced to their last sick extremity, absolutism is the only saving scheme. Pluralistic moralism simply makes their teeth chatter; it refrigerates the very heart within their breasts (293).
>
> We stand here before the final question of philosophy. . . . The monistic-pluralistic alternative [is] the deepest and most pregnant question that our minds can frame. Can it be that the disjunction is a final one?. . . . All I can say is that my own pragmatism offers no objection to my taking sides with the more moralistic view, and giving up the claim of total reconciliation. . . . In the end it is our faith and not our logic that decides such questions, and I deny the right of any pretended logic to veto my own faith (293–296).

In this dangerous universe, which may or may not be saved, James counts on the aid, not only of his fellow man, but also on a finite god or gods. We human beings stand in relation to the universe much as our canine and feline pets to us:

> They inhabit our drawing rooms and libraries. They take part in scenes of whose significance they have no inkling. They are merely tangent to curves of history the beginning and ends and forms of which pass wholly beyond their ken. So we are tangent to the wider life of things. . . . So we may well believe, on the proof that religious experience affords, that higher powers exist and are at work to save the world on ideal lines similar to our own (300).

Concluding Criticisms

Some of the criticisms made incidentally through the course of the exposition need not be repeated. Two of them, however, require repetition, yet only briefly. The brevity is not because of their small importance, but because of their utter destructiveness.

First, James has explicitly abandoned rational argumentation. He has denounced logic. The Absolutists used intellectualist logic to establish their position in the face of competing systems, but James was provoked that they then paid no attention to the same logic when it was used against themselves. Taken by itself this dissatisfaction would be a good reason for rejecting Absolutism; but when James claims the same privilege of disregarding logic, he loses whatever advantage his earlier arguments had given him.

In a similar instance, the logic that led him to reject monism calls for its replacement by theism. But theism is so intolerable to him that he discards logic. Either he would have to abandon "psychology without a soul," to which his whole scientific and Kantian education had committed him, or he would have to renounce logic and admit that life is irrational. He chose the latter alternative. "For my part," says James, "I have finally found myself compelled to give up the logic, fairly, squarely, and irrevocably."

This irrationalism is characteristic of much of the reaction against Hegel. Kierkegaard, Nietzsche, Durkheim, Dewey, and Ayer all oppose the law of contradiction. They subject the very forms of logic to evolutionary flux. They talk of logics that might have been or still may be, yet so different from ours as to be unimaginable. Perhaps in these logics, the assertion that all men are mortal will imply that no mortals are men. If we take such proposals as seriously as they seem to be meant, they become destructive of everything the authors have written. All their views, all their theses are left without rational foundation. No reason exists for agreeing with them. Such illogical talk puts an end to all rational discussion.

This intellectual suicide destroys James, Dewey, and Ayer *in toto* in one fell swoop. However, if the remainder of pragmatism does not require this irrationality (though it is doubtful that any of these authors can reinstate logic anywhere) one is curious about the value of such a remainder. Hence we shall proceed to further objections.

The second objection, if it does not apply to all the philosophers that fall under the previous objection, is equally sweeping for James himself. It is the objection Dewey made:

> Does Mr. James employ the pragmatic method to discover the value in terms of consequences in life of some formula which has its logical content already fixed; or does he employ it to criticize and revise and ultimately to constitute the meaning of that formula?

Dewey's perception is accurate. Passages have been quoted above in which James explicitly declares that the meaning of a formula is ultimately constituted by and of the experiences themselves. Yet other large sections can be understood only on an intellectualistic basis. When James describes his fervent belief in a "wider self from which saving experiences flow in," he can hardly be thinking of his own behavior as constituting this wider self. He needs his finite gods to support his meliorism. A superhuman consciousness must be more than James himself. He speaks of men as being internal parts of God. And all this occurs in a passage that stresses pluralism. The lack of consistency between the pure pragmatism of Dewey and these realistic, intellectualistic passages splits James's philosophy in two.

Since this second objection is as devastating as the first, for James if not for Dewey, the remainder of possible value for which we are searching must be sought in the non-Dewey half of James's philosophy. Purging James, therefore, of his pervasive inconsistency (so far as this is possible) we shall try to develop a massive objection to the morality and religion on which he bases his most characteristic positions.

What must be noticed first and always kept in mind is the fact that James's philosophy as a whole is based on his understanding of morality. True, he uses some intellectualistic arguments against Absolutism. These lead him to theism. But then his rejection of both theism and Absolutism, along with the discarding of logic, stems from the assumption that intimacy with the universe is not only desirable but is also a sufficient principle by which to choose between alternate worldviews. Another example of moral motivation is the division of mankind into tough-minded and tender-minded, into cynical and sympathetic: The one type chooses a materialistic philosophy, the other a spiritualistic; the one is pessimistic, the other optimistic. But James thinks that moral excellence lies in meliorism and for this reason chooses an intermediate position.

The crux of the matter, and the most vulnerable spot in James's proposals, is the choice he pictures God as offering to a man about to be created. Note that the choice does not lie between a world certain to be saved and a world certain to be lost. The choice James's God offers us lies between a world whose salvation is uncertain but possible and the slumber of nonentity.

Now is not this omission an error? If the constitution and destiny of the world are to be decided by our choice, by what right can James forbid us to consider any one of the most important possibilities? If God should say to a man, "You may choose certain salvation, uncertain salvation, or the slumber of nonentity," we might well guess that he would very probably choose certain salvation. Hence James's striking this choice from the ballot would seem to be a device for avoiding a large number of adverse votes.

Let us, however, without prejudice (as the legal saying is) study the choice James actually offers. God offers a world whose salvation is conditioned on each several agent doing his own level best. And James replies that every healthy-minded person would exclaim, *"Top! und schlag auf schlag."* Only a few morbid souls, Hindus and Buddhists who are afraid of life, men who are reduced to their last sick extremity—only these would refuse to be created.

One should note how important James considers this proposal. "We stand here before the final question of philosophy," he says. And therefore he cannot complain if judgment is rendered against him at this point.

Must not judgment be rendered against him? The condition of the world's salvation is that every human being shall do his level best to save the world. Otherwise it will be lost. Now the history of the world apparently provides instances of men who have not quite done their level best. Of course James did not know Hitler and Stalin, but he must have heard of Caligula and Nero, Louis XIV and Charles I, as well as Attila the Hun and earlier orientals. Whatever James may mean by a healthy-minded individual, it would seem that anyone with a modicum of prudence would decline this unpromising proposal. Such faith in man is surely misplaced, and the chance of salvation is infinitely remote.

James, in one place, says he is willing to lose, if only he can have the fun of living dangerously. But aside from the foolhardiness of such a choice, there is the added inconsistency that pragmatism praises that which works. If he should lose, it would be empirical proof that willingness to run the risk was wrong. Only success can justify pragmatism.

Of course, in addition to mankind, James counts on divine aid. There is a superhuman consciousness, a god or many gods that are supposed to help us. In this way the desperate situation might possibly be alleviated. It might, that is, if these gods really exist and if they are all interested in our salvation.

But what assurance do we have of these two redeeming factors? Even if we discount James's rejection of logic, is there an argument to prove that the gods exist? And second, if there are such gods, why must we think that all superhuman consciousnesses are good? Maybe, like men, not all the gods do their level best. In this case, whatever help one affords would be cancelled out by the disinclination of another.

Now, the trouble with James's theology is its complete lack of a reasonable basis. Toward the beginning of this monograph a letter to Henry W. Rankin was quoted in which James said,

> The mother sea and fountain head of all religions lie in the mystical experiences of the individual. . . . All theologies . . . are secondary growths superimposed; and the experiences make such

> flexible combinations . . . that one may almost say that they have no proper intellectual deliverance of their own. . . .

And yet it is only on the basis of these inarticulate experiences that we may believe in higher powers (*Pragmatism,* 300).

James's position, so it would seem—and pragmatism as a whole wherever accepted—has no base other than personal preference. This is a charge that pragmatists resent. John Dewey enters a vehement denial; Jacques Barzun toward the end of his entertaining *Darwin, Marx, and Wagner* brands it a complete misunderstanding. Yet can we credit these denials? At any rate James said, "In the end it is our faith and not our logic that decides such questions."

The evidence in James's case is quite clear. He prefers to live dangerously. He has a certain concept of healthy-mindedness. This is what he calls good. Conversely he has a distaste for Buddhism and morbid souls who do not prefer the foolhardy risks James enjoys. This caution, prudence, and wisdom he calls evil. But aside from his own baseless preference, he has no criterion for distinguishing good from evil. In spite of the fact that everything else he says depends on his personal morality, he really says nothing to recommend that morality to others. Hence his philosophy as a whole lacks support. This situation is not sufficient to convince a man with a different morality, with a morality that refuses to gamble against overwhelming odds. Surely, Christian theism is preferable to pragmatism.

John Dewey
1859–1952

1

INTRODUCTION

John Dewey was born in Vermont, studied in the University of Vermont, earned his doctor's degree at Johns Hopkins, and taught in the Universities of Michigan, Minnesota, Chicago, and in Columbia University from 1904 to his retirement in 1929. Both before and after retirement Dewey published voluminously. There were many educational writings; *A Common Faith* gives his opinions on religion; a volume is devoted to aesthetics; *Human Nature and Conduct, Logic, the Theory of Inquiry,* and *The Quest for Certainty,* as well as many other titles, expound his basic philosophy. Since his biography is almost completely academic—teaching and publication—it is possible to begin the present study in *medias res.*

The philosophy of John Dewey, varied as it is in its particulars, may like that of the Stoics be comprehended under three headings. Philosophy, said the Stoics, is like an egg: The white is ethics, the yolk is physics, and logic is the shell; or again, philosophy is like an animal: Logic corresponds to the bones and sinews, ethics to the flesh, and physics to the soul. This account therefore will be divided into three parts: physics, ethics, and logic. The first part will be the shortest, for it must not be supposed that Dewey was a physicist. Though his respect for the particular achievements of science was pronounced and profound, his chief interest centered in scientific method. It was by this method that he hoped to solve the pressing problems of ethics, politics, and sociology. Hence an exposition of Dewey's philosophy cannot spend much time on science proper, but after the method is stated must pass on to its application. The second section of this discussion will concern ethics, or, more broadly, the social sciences. Some examples of Dewey's concrete proposals will be given, but of course the important thing is his attempt to show how such problems can be solved by scientific experimentation. Then, finally, in the third place, just as his account of science merges immediately with questions of ethics, so his scientific ethics cannot long be kept separate from a theory of logic.

Though the subjects merge, for they are intended to merge, criticism may well try to separate them a little. Perhaps Dewey's views of science are tenable while his ethics is poor; or the main outlines of his ethics could be commendable though his science might be mistaken. To be sure, if his ethics should prove indefensible, Dewey would be the first to admit that nothing much of value would be left. But finally—however plausible his science and ethics might be—if the logic on which the whole depends cannot withstand criticism, if the shell of the egg is broken, if the bones of the animal are dissolved, nothing whatever will survive.

2

SCIENCE

Dewey viewed modern society as frustrated by reason of an inconsistent adherence to two conflicting ideals. Inherited from the Greeks is an esteem of theory and a disdain of practice, a spectator theory of knowledge, a withdrawal into the ivory tower. This ideal has been enforced by religious approval of spiritual contemplation as well as by the self-sufficient rationalism of absolute idealism. On the other hand, modern science, by its experimental methods, by its manipulation of physical bodies, and by its practical applications, has contributed to our control of nature and to our ease and comfort. Though we may be ashamed to confess that such materialistic developments are our ultimate goals and may pay an amount of lip service to Greek and Christian ideals, we continue to direct most of our energies in the modern direction. This is not only a split between what we say and what we do. It also involves two inconsistent methods of procedure. Our professed values are based on the non-empirical philosophies of the past, while our daily lives are controlled by practice and experiment. Thus modern science effected a breach between our daily interests and our faith concerning eternal destiny and the nature of ultimate reality. Therefore the chief problem of contemporary philosophy is to unify man's divided views of value and nature. The astounding success of experimental science in the limited fields it has taken over is the promise of effecting integration in the wider field of collective human experience (*The Quest for Certainty*, 24ff., 225; *Reconstruction in Philosophy*, 42; *Experience and Nature*, 394).

The total situation, however, is not quite so simple as these few lines seem to make it, for modern science, or better, modern scientific theory, has actually contributed to the aggravation of the difficulty. The philosophic version of the popular conflict between science and religion is the charge, the substantial charge, that science has denuded the universe of all value. When Galileo turned attention from the qualities of bodies and initiated a quantitative study, he laid the foundation of a view that reduced hot, cold, sweet, and sour to "secondary" qualities existing only in the mind and not in the real world. Obviously, values were even less real. The real world then became an infinite darkness where dead matter is moved by insensate forces. When science is thought to reach ultimate reality, and when it is thought not to reach values, then science is said to eliminate values (*The Quest for Certainty,* 94–102). This untenable result, a valid inference from Galileo and Newton, arose from these two mistaken notions of the nature of science and the function of experimentation. If, however, science does not disclose the real nature of antecedent being, but is understood operationally, values can be saved, experimentation extended, and the modern conflict between competing ideals can be resolved.

Whatever may be the flaw in the Newtonian philosophy of science, it is not reliance on experimentation. Aristotle observed, but the modern scientist experiments. Instead of merely contemplating an object and hoping to discover its fixed and characteristic "form," a physicist or chemist operates on it. He grinds it or dissolves it; he passes an electric current through it; he heats it or freezes it; in short, he does things to it. If the astronomer cannot manipulate the stars, he can at least operate on their light, pass it through prisms, or bat it back and forth with mirrors (*Reconstruction in Philosophy,* 113; *The Quest for Certainty,* 87). The immediate purpose of these operations is to study changes. Instead of trying to define something that remains constant in the changes, the scientist searches for constant relations among the changes (*Reconstruction in Philosophy,* 61; *The Quest for Certainty,* 102). The further purpose of science is a system of interconnected changes; and though reading a barometer may not prevent unwanted rain, it enables us to change our relation to the rain by planting a garden, carrying an umbrella, or altering the course of a ship. By a knowledge of correlated changes, therefore, we can control or produce the qualities we desire. Arid lands can be irrigated, or drinking water can be produced from the ocean (*The Quest for Certainty*, 98, 196, 128–132).

This emphasis on control for purposes of non-cognitive experience indicates that science, instead of giving us knowledge of antecedent realities, rather constructs new objects of knowledge. Or, simply, science constructs objects of knowledge. The old objects—the common things: rain, salt, lead, stars—are qualitative objects of enjoyment. Science expresses their changes in quantitative or mathematical form. This makes the old objects candidates for receiving new qualities and means for serving new ends. Natural objects no longer have fixed ends of their own. But so far as knowledge is concerned, as distinct from enjoyment, it is the experiment itself—the results of planned operations—that "form the objects that have the property of being *known*" (*The Quest for Certainty*, 86–87, 99, 103).

The distinction between cognitive and non-cognitive experience, the effect of experiment in constructing objects of knowledge, as well as the control and production of desired qualities, is further clarified by Dewey's view of what a scientific concept really is. A concept is not a piece of information about independent, antecedent being. It is not a revelation that reality is denuded of secondary qualities. On the contrary, scientific concepts are plans of action. For example, the analysis of water into H_2O does not deny that water is wet and that it quenches thirst. Water is all that common experience says it is. However, the term *water* does not connect the common stuff with ice and steam. The chemical formula not only expresses these relationships but also relates water to other chemicals. Thus the scientific concept, as a part of a developed chemical theory, is essentially a statement of how to produce water, hydrogen, oxygen, or other desired compounds (*The Quest for Certainty*, 158–159).

More generally, a concept is defined by operations. Mass is not the quantity of matter; it is the set of operations used when one works with this factor in a formula. *Length* means the motions one goes through when measuring. This operationalism gives ideas an empirical origin, not in the old sense of a passive reception of sensory qualities, but in the experimental sense of acts to be performed. Sensory qualities have their importance, no doubt, but only as consequences of intentional action. Qualities are ends to be produced. The concept is the method of production; it is a statement, not of what is or has been, but of acts to be performed (*The Quest for Certainty,* 112, 131, 137).

Newton was too metaphysical; his empiricism was defective. He believed that permanent particles were necessary to explain nature. Although he claimed sensory grounds for assuming the existence of atoms and gave them no properties other than those belonging to all the bodies of sensory experience, the belief that non-observable permanents are needed to prevent a collapse into chaos is the result of a metaphysical, non-empirical fear (*The Quest for Certainty,* 116). Likewise his independent framework of space and time is metaphysical, though the scientific difficulties of observing simultaneous motions was only recently appreciated. Long ago, Newton's principles had been attacked logically. His assumption that a particle and a velocity can be determined in isolation from other particles and velocities is incompatible with his other assumption of the continuous interaction of all particles. At first this made no observational difference. Then the Michelson-Morley experiment uncovered a discrepancy between the velocity of light and the theory of dynamics. Newton had thought it possible to determine the simultaneity of two events even when they are not in the same observational field. Einstein demanded what Newton could not furnish: an empirical method for determining simultaneity. Since this was not forthcoming, Einstein kept the experiment but altered the concepts. This resulted in the abolition of Newton's absolutes and the formation of concepts by actual operations. When operations change, as they constantly do with advancing experimentation, the concepts must change too (*The Quest for Certainty,* 142–146, 202–206).

This is perhaps about as much as can be said of Dewey's philosophy of science without proceeding to its ethical applications or its foundation in the more general theory of instrumentalism. Inasmuch as the present study will conclude with severe criticism of

Dewey, it ought to be said here that operationalism in physics does not necessarily stand or fall with Dewey's use of it in general. Perhaps this is a thoroughly tenable view of science. Chemical formulas may give us no knowledge of antecedent being. Perhaps space and time, as physical concepts, are nothing more than a set of motions in a laboratory. At any rate, the rapidity with which scientific theories of the recent past have been invented, accepted, and discarded warns us that science is not fixed and absolute truth. Newtonian science lasted two centuries. Today's science hardly lasts two decades. Operationalism is a very plausible description of what science in actual practice is. But whether operationalism and the general theory of instrumentalism can provide a solid basis for ethics is an entirely different question. To prepare for an answer to this question, it is necessary to give a rather careful account of Dewey's opinions on ethics and values.

3

ETHICS

Since an abstract analysis of value might prove to be a confusing introduction to Dewey's ethical speculations, a random selection of his concrete proposals for politics, economics, and morality will first be made. These will show what Dewey wishes to justify by his underlying method. Then the method of justification can be more intelligently discussed.

Sampling of Opinions

As a first example of Dewey's specific recommendations, his opposition to capital punishment is instructive. A theory of justice, he argues (*Human Nature and Conduct,* Chapter I), which demands the vindication of the law irrespective of instruction and reform of the wrongdoer is as much a refusal to recognize responsibility as is the sentimental gush which makes a suffering victim out of a criminal. That capital punishment ignores responsibility depends on the idea that society is about as much to blame for the murder as is the murderer. The committing of murder, evidently, is not so horrible a crime as to destroy the criminal's right to live; and, accordingly, criminal law can seek only the rehabilitation of the offender.

A second example concerns his educational theories, of which a fair hint is also found in the same book (*Human Nature and Conduct,* Chapter II, Section 2). Parents teach children to conform to custom because they distrust the child's intelligence. The moral habits so taught become deeply ingrained and govern later conscious thought. These infantilisms are most "un-get-at-able" just where critical thought is most needed—namely, in morals, religion, and politics. Unfortunately these irrationalities are very numerous, and if one were to list them and call for their eradication, Dewey admits, one would probably be ousted from respectable society. Thus it would seem that Dewey's morals were considerably different from what was respectable during the period in which he lived.

Some of his political tendencies are indicated in the next-to-last chapter of the same book. He rejects liberal principles (as is common with twentieth-century "liberals") and urges governmental regulation. "Find a man," he says, "who believes that all men need is freedom *from* oppressive legal and political measures, and you have a man who, unless he is merely obstinately maintaining his own private privileges, carries at the back of his head some heritage of the metaphysical doctrine of free will, plus an optimistic confidence in natural harmony" (*Human Nature and Conduct,* Chapter IV, Section 3). This sentence doubtless distorts the truth. Probably no one says that freedom from oppression is *all* a man needs, yet this does not make such freedom any the less desirable. Dewey uses the invidious terms *obstinacy* and *private privilege* rather than the concept of inalienable personal rights. Further, some people oppose totalitarianism, not because they believe in free will, nor because they are optimistic, but because they believe in human depravity. They think that men cannot be trusted with too much power. In any case, Dewey's preference for government controls is clear. He has no theoretical objection to coercion, for he goes on to say that whether a man should be compelled to join a labor union against his will is not a matter of principle, but an experimental matter to be decided scientifically by concrete consequences. Since, however, the coercer and the victim will obviously place different evaluations on the consequences, it becomes a major question requiring later examination how such concrete consequences can determine what ought and what ought not to be done.

The tenor of these passages is reproduced any number of times. Every so often, specific philosophic controversies are solved by social bias. For example, the theory of fixed natural laws, he says, has retarded social advance, for it considers government regulation as interference. Indeed, it would seem that science in general is not controlled by class interests, and therefore society should be reconstructed (*The Quest for Certainty*, 79 ff., 210). Calling for extensive control over individuals (*Problems of Men*, 160–163), if he does not actually impugn the honesty of his opponents, at least he speaks somewhat roughly. He attacks the "clamorous assertion" of "those who have enjoyed the power and regulation of other human beings because of the existing set-up in political, ecclesiastical, and economic institutions," and then asks, "Shall we have reason for believing that their concern for human values is honest?" One may well pause to compare this objection to the regulation of other human beings with Dewey's own demand for a scientific theory of the causes of desire so that we can make men have the "right" desires and manipulate them as we now manipulate physical things (*Problems of Men*, 178–179).

In *A Common Faith* Dewey gives his main ideas on religion. Essentially, religion is an attempt to adjust to the actual situations of life, and these valuable experiences should be emancipated from the historical forms of organized religions which are repellent to the modern mind. Since the situation changes from age to age, religion should also change. Doctrinal, intellectual, and institutional features are adventitious accretions. Perhaps it should not be said that religion is identical with morality, for morality must include a number of lesser everyday responsibilities, whereas religion is a concern for inclusive ideals that produce self-integration and introduce perspective in the shifting episodes of existence. If few people have much religious ardor, the fault lies not so much in the power of ideals as in the dissipation of such power into supernatural fancies irrelevant to actual life. This attitude obscures the distinctively religious values inherent in natural experience. Therefore, these real values should be divorced from creeds and cults, for these values are not bound up with any item of intellectual assent such as the existence of God. The details of religion must be sought through the only gateway to knowledge that there is, namely, science. Scientific knowledge may be constantly changing, but there is no other source of knowledge. Or, more accurately, science is not a body of fixed knowledge: It is a method. This does not rule out God, for *God* may be defined as the unity of all ideals that arouse desire and action. Any other conception of God—transcendental or supernatural—is merely an appeal to force, for all that supernatural existence can add to the reality of ideals is the power to punish and reward. There is also the added difficulty of the problem of evil.

Such themes, taken from *A Common Faith,* raise again the question asked just above: How can science determine in the concrete what is ideal and what is not? With the recurrence of this question there is no point in continuing these introductory samplings of Dewey's opinions. It is now time to begin a more systematic exposition of his ethical theory.

The Place of Ethics in Pragmatism

Although every complete system of philosophy must include an account of ethics, one system may assign it a greater importance than another. In the Aristotelian system ethics is a relatively minor factor. Christianity, however, with its condemnation of sin and its call to righteousness places a strong emphasis on morality. Nevertheless, ethics is not the basis of the Christian system. Theology is more fundamental, for ethics depends on God. Sin is lawlessness, moral principles are the commands of God, and practical obedience to them depends on divine grace. In contrast with both Aristotelianism and Christianity, Dewey's instrumentalism has a far more desperate need of ethics. Instrumentalism, it might be said, is nothing but ethics. It has been hinted that ethics is based on science; but the underlying pragmatic logic, which makes science and truth the results of deliberative action, returns us to practical ends as the humanistic court of last resort. "The effective condition of the integration of all divided purposes and conflicts of belief is the realization that intelligent action is the sole ultimate resource of mankind in every field whatsoever" (*The Quest for Certainty,* 252). There is no God from whom man can obtain comfort, encouragement, and strength;

much less wisdom, instruction, and intervention. Man has only himself.

It is this atheism that throws into relief the desperate need of an irrefragable theory of ethics. If humanism fails to save man from the plight of his conflicts in every field whatsoever, humanism fails indeed. It may have an admirable theory of science, it may devise effective aids in education, it may stimulate professors to take part in politics; but since science and politics are only means to chosen ends and ideals, if humanism cannot rationally justify one ideal as against another, if its theory of ethics cannot give clear-cut guidance in the perplexities of life, it will have failed in its main endeavor and must be abandoned.

Pragmatic Flux in Ethics

Whatever ideals or standards Dewey may propose, they are not to be regarded as fixed and final norms for all human beings. One quotation will suffice for the moment:

> We institute standards of justice, truth, esthetic quality, etc. . . . exactly as we set up a platinum bar as a standard measurer of lengths. The standard is just as much subject to modification and revision in the one case as in the other on the basis of the consequences of its operational application. . . . The superiority of one conception of justice to another is of the same order as the superiority of the metric system. . . although not of the same quality (*Logic, the Theory of Inquiry*, 216).

It will soon become clear that this comparison between a standard of justice and a standard of measurement is not an adequate illustration. A given line is always longer than a second line, whether we use inches or centimeters to measure them; and a weight is always heavier than another, be it in grams or ounces. In morals, however, an act may be commendable on one standard and evil on another. This is a point that must be watched throughout the following analysis.

For Dewey's purposes another illustration is better. Moral standards are like language in that both are the result of custom. Theories of absolute ethics argue that ideal standards antecede customs and judge of their rightness or wrongness; any alleged ideals that are merely the result of custom could not be its judge. That this absolutism is at best unnecessary is seen in the case of language. There were no antecedent principles of grammar. Language evolved from unintelligent babblings and instinctive gestures. Then came the rules of grammar and the apparatus of literacy. This, however, is not the end, for the language and its grammar change to meet new situations and new needs. Words change their forms and meanings, new expressions are invented, and the old rules become archaic. Nevertheless the rules of language, though merely the unforeseen and unintended results of custom, exercise their authority over us. Grammar and morals are both a part of life. No one can escape them, even if he wants to. Man's choice is simply between adopting more or less significant customs (*Human Nature and Conduct,* I, 5).

This analogy between the rules of grammar and the principles of morality carries important implications. Most obvious is the fact that different nations use different languages. Of course, if we wish to speak French, we must conform to its customs sufficiently to be understood. And if we are born French, we do not have much choice at first. Eventually, however, it may become possible to emigrate to the United States. This involves a decision to speak English rather than French. The opportunity to disapprove of the moral customs of a nation and, against social pressure, live a different kind of life is more readily available than emigration. Does not this require a moral norm superior to the customs that are condemned?

Dewey's analogy with language tends to minimize the importance of this question. After all, it is of no great moment whether a person speaks French, German, or English, nor whether he breaks a few rules of grammar in doing so. But Christian missionaries report that in certain sections of Africa social customs are such that girls scarcely reach their teens before they have been raped half a dozen times. And it was only last century that there were cannibal tribes on several Pacific islands. The missionaries opposed these "moral standards," these products of custom, and these instinctive gestures. They held that there are divinely revealed, fixed, and universal standards that condemn such actions. Now, if this is not true, and if ethics is analogous to language, can there be any justification for imposing the customs of one society upon another society? Does not the condemnation of one set of customs require a norm that is more than the effect of another set of customs?

Dewey has an interesting and perhaps a disturbing answer to this question. In the first place, he asserts that the proponents of fixed standards, such as Christian missionaries, are self-deceived. They have, in fact, no absolute norm. Their moral ideas are merely the results of the customs of their own group. Custom, therefore, is still the source of all morality. Now, in the second place, the opposition of one custom to a wider custom is a form of class warfare; indeed, "the most serious form of class warfare." Class warfare is not overscrupulous. Each side treats its opponent as a willful violator of absolute moral principles. Thus we have the present conflict between the bourgeoisie and the proletariat. Hence the notion of fixed moral standards results in a war that can be ended only by force. Apparently, rape remains commendable in Africa.

The absence of fixed truth in science and the instrumental theory of logic will be discussed in the proper order, but that there are no eternal and universal principles of morality so permeates pragmatism that further summaries and documentation are unnecessary. *Reconstruction in Philosophy,* chapter five, bases the tentativeness of ethics on the tentativeness of science; and the whole of the *Quest for Certainty,* a will-o'-the-wisp pursued by traditional philosophers, offers as its substitute the scientific promise of security.

Values

The immediate problem therefore is to identify values and ideals in the flux of experience. John Dewey believed that he had seen the problem clearly and that he had discovered the key to its solution. The deepest problem of modern life, so he held, is the integration of man's beliefs about the physical world with his beliefs about human values. In the Middle Ages, science and religion were harmonious because they were both developed against a single philosophical background. All problems were solved on Thomistic principles. Today, however, medieval science has disappeared, but common beliefs about value still retain some medieval flavor. Since, now, modern conduct is mainly motivated by modern science, the result is that the conduct of modern man conflicts with his beliefs about values. Because of two reactions to this conflict, two disadvantages arise. Some men with a strong emotional attachment to the antiquated theory of value disparage and retard science, at least by dissipating their energies in unfruitful endeavors (*The Quest for Certainty*, 35–36). The other type accepts science wholeheartedly, but because the values they have been taught cannot be scientifically established, they repudiate value altogether. Therefore, the important problem for a philosophy that does not wish to be isolated from modern life is to harmonize modern theory and practice.

The solution of this problem is to be found in a more thorough exploitation of scientific method. As science detached problem after problem from the medieval synthesis, its successes accumulated until now in the twentieth century there is reason to suppose that all the problems of humanity are amenable to the same method. Beliefs about values, about ethics and sociology, are today in much the same state as were beliefs about physics in the prescientific era (*Reconstruction in Philosophy*, 42–43). What is needed is the application of scientific techniques. Only two attitudes block the acceptance of this view. With some there is a basic distrust of the capacity of experience to develop standards, ideals, or norms for life. This first attitude depends on eternal values and appeals to a Supreme

Being. No hope can be expected from such a theistic view. Secular interests now dominate men's minds; the sense of transcendental values has become enfeebled; the authority of the church has diminished; men may profess the old religion, but they act secularly. This divergence between what men do and what they say is the outward evidence of the conflict in modern thought. To solve the problem and remove the conflict, men's thoughts should be made to conform to what they do: They play golf on Sunday and believe in the existence of God; while continuing to play golf, they should be taught to repudiate belief in God, rather than to change their conduct and go to church.

The second attitude which blocks acceptance of the scientific method is the enjoyment of pleasures, goods, or values irrespective of the method used to produce this enjoyment. Such a view supposes that "to be enjoyed and to be a value are two names for one and the same fact" (*The Quest for Certainty*, 258). This attitude or theory of value is superior to the theistic view in that the values are concrete experiences of desire and satisfaction here and now. Its failure arises from the fact that these enjoyments are casual and unregulated by intelligence. Escape from transcendental absolutism is not to be had in casual enjoyments, but in defining value by enjoyments which are the consequences of intelligent action. "Without the intervention of thought, enjoyments are not values but problematic goods, becoming values when they reissue in a changed form from intelligent behavior" (*The Quest for Certainty*, 259).

Casual Enjoyments

A passage from an earlier book had already explained this view, except that in the earlier passage Dewey uses the term *value* in a broader sense and had not restricted it as he did in the *Quest for Certainty*. Here (*Experience and Nature*, 396) the term *value* is the equivalent of the later term *enjoyment* or *problematic good*. In the following summary, Dewey's usage will be preserved.

Values, therefore, are fugitive and precarious so that there is needed a method of discriminating among goods on the basis of their conditions and consequences. Values are just values with certain intrinsic qualities; of them as values there is nothing to be said: They are simply what they are. Whatever can be said of them pertains to their causes and effects. The reason for enjoying a value is often that the object is a means to or a result of something else; the reason concerns the cause of the value and has nothing to do with intrinsic value-quality.

Before continuing the summary, one should stop to note a confusing factor in the lines above. True it is that values are often enjoyed, or at least chosen, because they are causes of something else. Such values, by some authors, are called instrumental as opposed to intrinsic values; they range from taking a cab to the airport to visiting the dentist. But Dewey's argument really requires that this be the case, not just "often," but always. Let us stop and ask whether all values are instrumental, or whether some are intrinsic. Is it true that the reason for enjoying a value has nothing to do with the intrinsic value-quality? This question should be kept in mind as the summary proceeds.

A genuine good, Dewey continues, differs from a spurious good because of reflection on consequences. All criticism concerns consequences because no properties carry adequate credentials on their face.

In this connection two points should be raised. The first, mentioned a few lines above, concerns the antecedents of which the value in question is a consequence. This point has to do with the enjoyment of casual pleasures irrespective of the method used to produce them. The second and perhaps more important point touches on the consequences which the value itself produces.

To invent an example, suppose that a man applies for a job, does his work, and is paid; in such a case, the money is not a spurious good but a real value because it was earned by intelligent action. Had the man found the same amount of money on the sidewalk, it would not have been a real value. So Dewey contends. To most people, however, money found is just as valuable as money earned. In fact, although the purchasing powers of a dollar earned and of a dollar found are the same, the work of earning may be so lengthy and laborious that the sum of a life's values are diminished by intelligent foresight and increased by a lucky find. The workman's time and strength might well be so exhausted that what the dollar buys could barely be enjoyed. Thus one might say, in sharp contrast with Dewey, that the casual, unearned enjoyment is the greater value.

Of course, if Dewey meant merely that it is not wise to depend for one's living on finding money in the street, his argument would be sound enough, but it would be trivial. A theist of the most pronounced supernatural views, as well as the Epicurean who tries to avoid trouble by dozing in the sun, would agree that a certain amount of planning and work are necessary for our ordinary satisfactions. This triviality cannot be the basis of Dewey's antagonism to theists and Epicureans. His expressions and emphasis seem to say that unexpected enjoyments are simply of no value. They are spurious.

This view, which seems so odd to common sense, apparently depends on the thesis that the value of an object depends on its being a result of and a means to something else and, in particular, does not depend on its intrinsic enjoyable quality. Nothing is valuable in itself. Enough has been said now of the antecedents of the enjoyment; the second point concerns the consequences of the enjoyed value.

Intrinsic Quality

On this point, too, the criticism—continuing to press the issue of intrinsic value—will be much the same. It may be granted that we assign value to money because of the possible consequences, namely, the things we can buy with it; in this sense a bill or a check, being only a piece of paper, does not carry value credentials on its face. But is this to say that nothing does? Is there nothing valuable for itself alone? Are all values merely instrumental? Is there no final end whatever?

For purposes of illustration, a game of chess will do. Is the pleasure of chess dependent for its value on the consequences? Of course, chess may be used to cement friendships, and no doubt other consequences could be ingeniously listed. But ordinarily, the reason for playing chess is not at all that the game is a means to or a result of something else. On the contrary, it has all to do with its intrinsic value-quality. If the credentials on its face were not adequate, chess would not be chosen.

Dewey, in strange company with Aristotle, might spurn this illustration of chess. Playing games is not a sufficiently serious activity to be commensurate with major human endeavors. Besides, as Aristotle said, recreation is for the sake of work: we play in order to work, we do not work in order to play. Although such sentiments fit the Aristotelian viewpoint very well, it is not so clear that Dewey can use them with much consistency. If nothing is intrinsically valuable, how could one insist that play is a means to work rather than the reverse? If nothing carries its own credentials, how could one distinguish between the serious and the trivial? Aristotle made recreation a means to an intrinsically valuable activity, an activity that is chosen for its own sake and not as a means to anything else. But if, as Dewey says, there is no final cause, and if everything is chosen merely as a means to something else and never because of its intrinsic qualities, does it make any difference what we choose?

Young men and women in large numbers choose to go to college. On Dewey's theory, only too well accepted by the students, the reason cannot be any intrinsic value in knowledge. To give such a reason would be to flee from reality and take refuge in the discredited Aristotelian ivory tower. For the young man, college is a means of getting a better job; for the young woman, it is a means of getting a better man. But neither the family that marriage brings nor the food that the job supplies is to be chosen for any intrinsic quality. These, too, are merely means to something else. College is the means to a job; a job is the means to marriage; marriage is the means to a family; a family, along with the job, is the means of sending a son to college. But chess is the means of restricting social contacts to a small number; restricting social contacts is the means of avoiding marriage; single blessedness saves the money one would spend on a son's tuition; and this money is the means for purchasing a more handsome set of chess men. But why follow one causal series rather than the other? All activities are valueless means to other valueless means. The means have no end, and choice has become irrational. Or, at least, choices are based on nothing else than personal preference.

Here it would seem that another humanist, Gardner Williams, sees more clearly than John Dewey when he writes, "It does not matter, from an individual's point of view, how he is satisfied, so long as, in the long run, he is satisfied."* In this context the *how* seems to include both the presence or absence of intelligent foresight and the identification of what satisfies.

To these last assertions, Dewey would probably reply with some expressions of disgust. Such opinions he would repudiate, not merely as a lack of enthusiasm for scientific method, but also as an avoidance of responsibility for reconstructing economic, political, and religious institutions. In a number of places, Dewey bases his rejection of opposing theories on sociological preferences. Epistemology, for example, wastes time that could profitably be spent in remedying social evils. Thought should not be employed for any private good; if it aims at some special result, it is not sincere (*Reconstruction in Philosophy,* 124, 126). Strange to say, in this context he even speaks of "something worth while for itself," though on the next page he adds with more consistency, "there is no particular end set up in advance so as to shut in the activities of observation, forming of ideas, and application." Instead of

> emotional satisfaction and private comfort, . . . the satisfaction in question means a satisfaction of the needs and conditions of the problem out of which the idea, the purpose and method of action arises. . . . So repulsive is a conception of truth which

*Gardner Williams, *Humanistic Ethics,* 55.

> makes it a mere tool of private ambition and aggrandizement that the wonder is that critics have attributed such a notion to sane men (*Reconstruction in Philosophy*, 157).

But is Dewey's disgust a sufficient reply to the objections? His political aims will be taken up later. Here the question is, by what logical argument can Dewey recommend college rather than chess? Has he any reason for being disgusted at private good? He cannot rightly claim that critics have mistakenly attributed crazy notions to sane men. Professor Williams is a sane man; so were the Sophists and the Epicureans. And many other men will refuse to relinquish particular ends, private comfort, and intrinsic goods merely because Dewey finds them repulsive.

Certainty or Security

Behind Dewey's disgust and behind the insistence that the methods of science will solve ethical problems lies a contrast that Dewey was fond of emphasizing. It is the contrast between certainty and security. Religionists, mystics, and deluded Platonists seek for certainty and sometimes claim that they have actually come into possession of absolute truth. But the instrumentalist theory of science and F.C.S. Schiller's keen criticism of Plato show that fixed truth cannot be had. The traditional desire for certainty should therefore be abandoned. In its place modern science has provided something much better—security. Chemistry improves the food supply of civilized peoples. Physics allows for the invention of telephones, radio, and jet planes. If, now, we study the conditions by which values can be made more secure and more ample, we have solved, so Dewey seems to say, the problems of ethics.

It used to be thought—and even scientists of the modern era, for example, Newton—have thought that science is a discovery of truth. Water, they said, really is H_2O. This is a mistaken view of the nature and purpose of science. Science does not discover what has been; science produces what will be. H_2O is not water; H_2SO_4 is not sulfuric acid. These are formulas, plans of action, by which we make use of water and sulfuric acid for useful purposes. By such chemical formulas it becomes possible to produce sulfuric acid, or hydrogen gas from water. Similarly, all the laws of science are essentially plans of action, plans for controlling nature, plans for securing the future. There is no knowledge of antecedent being, but scientific method can control and manipulate nature so as to make our goods secure (*The Quest for Certainty,* 39, 42, 128; *Experience and Nature,* 396).

That Plato and Aristotle, Descartes and Spinoza, and even Newton failed to reach absolute truth in science is a plausible and an inescapable conclusion from Dewey's arguments; Schiller's were still more convincing. The quest for certainty may have indeed been a failure. But if the failure of these rationalists is a reason for abandoning hope of truth, is it a reason for adopting a hope of security?

Dewey asserts that modern scientific method can solve the problem of ethics. But is this problem the problem of security? Is it not rather the choice of what to secure? Dewey has indicated some rather definite political choices. He opposes *laissez-faire,* liberty, and individualism, and advocates some type of collectivism. Yet we are forced to ask whether the scientific method or his theory compels us to choose the one rather than the other.

Of course, we might also ask whether science can secure the ideal once it has been chosen. In this barbaric twentieth century, politicians promise security and scientists devise means for making it impossible. One widely acclaimed demagogue promised his nation freedom from fear. Since then, scientific fear has gripped the whole world. Science seems to have secured man's destruction more than, or at least as much as, it has secured his preservation. At best, science can secure one ideal about as easily as another. Dictatorship and republicanism can both make use of it. It furnishes means to whatever a man may choose. But can it furnish any reason for choosing this in preference to that? The main question therefore is not how to secure values but how to select them. To substitute security for certainty under these conditions must be an act of philosophic and existential desperation.

However, security, reflection on conditions and consequences, and the disparagement of intrinsic qualities are a consistent application of the parallelism of ethics with science. Science turned its back on the immediately perceived wetness of water in order to form a conception, H_2O, that could produce more secure and more significant experiences of the wetness. Things enjoyed should be treated similarly; they are possibilities of values to be achieved. To say that something is enjoyed is equivalent to saying water is wet. This may be a fact, but it is not a value. A value is something satisfactory, and the satisfactory is that which *will do,* i.e., a prediction concerning the future, not a statement about the present. A statement about the present, such as, this experience is satisfying, only raises a problem. Granted that we enjoy it, how is the enjoyment to be rated? Is it a value or not? Is it something *to be* enjoyed? To say that it is a value means that it will continue to satisfy. It *will* do. A statement of present fact makes no claim on action, but a judgment about what is *to be* desired looks to the future and possesses *de jure* and not merely *de facto* quality.

De Jure Value

In the light of previous ethical speculation, the distinction between a merely *de facto* quality and a *de jure* quality would seem to be an important one. Is it possible to see that one enjoyment will not do and that another will do? How can we distinguish the value that will continue to satisfy in the future from the one that will not? And how can this distinction be made without private comforts and final ends?

Dewey notes that although values must be connected inherently with likings, preferences, or desires, they are not to be connected with any random preference, but only with those rationally approved after examination. The conflict between thoughtless, sporadic wishes and plans reflectively chosen for long-term purposes is a common one. About the first, people usually say, I would *like* to do or have this; but about the second they assert, with regret or determination, I *ought* to do that. Dewey must take into account the "ought" of traditional morality, and the distinction between *de jure* and *de facto* is to the point. The question is whether instrumentalism can justify such a distinction. What sort of examination will reveal that one liking is to be approved and other rejected? And inasmuch as Dewey criticizes the rationalistic theory on the score that it affords no guidance (*The Quest for Certainty,* 264–267), one naturally expects that Dewey will provide the guidance.

What sort of examination Dewey has in mind is clear enough—at least it is easy to quote the sentences by which Dewey believes he has met the requirements. In fact he puts one of them in italics:

> *Judgments about values are judgments about the conditions and the results of experienced objects; judgments about that which should regulate the formation of our desires, affections, and enjoyments* (*The Quest for Certainty,* 265).

When duties or values conflict, dogmatism attempts to construct a scale of values. But this, says Dewey, is a confession of inability to judge the concrete. The alternative to a hierarchical scheme is judgment by means of the relations in which values occur. One must examine their causes, conditions, and consequences, their interactions and connections; the more we ascertain of these details, the more we know the objects in question, and the better we can judge their value.

What could be more plausible, more in accord with common sense? But as understood by superficial common sense, does it support Dewey's position? If Dewey had meant merely that an adequate example of some immediate enjoyment or casual preference requires a look at the probable consequences, he would be doing no more than refuting Billy Bones. Captain William Bones in Admiral Benbow Inn preferred more rum, but its value or disvalue is seen in his speedy death. However, it appears that Dewey used this type of examination, not merely as a necessary but as a sufficient criterion of value. He states:

> Enjoyments that issue from conduct directed by insight into relations have a meaning and a validity due to the way in which they are experienced. Such enjoyments are not to be repented of; they generate no aftertaste of bitterness (*The Quest for Certainty*, 267).

In the case of Billy Bones most of us would decide that rum was a disvalue because its relations, conditions, and consequences involved death. But Billy Bones apparently thought that life without rum was worse than death. The mere examination and listing of causes and consequences does not ensure agreement on value. The early Christian martyrs knew the consequence of refusal to deny their faith, and they chose death more deliberately than Captain Bones. Are we to say that since the pirate and the martyrs both examined the relations, interactions, causes, and conditions, their enjoyments are equally *de jure* values with no aftertaste of bitterness? And will Dewey admit that their choices are as satisfactory as his?

Dewey's argument here depends on three related assumptions: that casual enjoyments are not values, that values are means to ends, and that enjoyments chosen in the light of their relations are not to be repented of. He gives an example. Heating and lighting, speed of transportation and communication, have been attained, not by lauding their desirability, but by studying their conditions. "Knowledge of relations having been obtained, ability to produce followed, and enjoyment ensued as a matter of course" (*The Quest for Certainty*, 269).

If this example is intended to show how scientific method can produce ideals, solve the problem of ethics, and secure goods—and such seems to be the intention of the example; if, that is, this example is supposed to answer the previous criticisms—it is not convincing. Scientific method undoubtedly secures speed of transportation, but enjoyment and satisfaction do not follow as a matter of course. Speed of transportation and communication help to make war more horrible. Knowledge of relations and ability to produce can be directed toward painful ends as easily as toward pleasurable ends. In both cases the means are valuable for the production of the ends; and in both cases the agent may have an exhaustive knowledge of causes, conditions, consequences, interactions, and connections; but will Dewey admit that therefore one course of action is as valuable as the other? Can he maintain that efficiency *per se* is the ultimate reason for making a choice?

A shabbily clad character managed to get past the doorman of a swank hotel and made his way to the mezzanine. There the house detective found him and booted him down the stairs into the lobby. The doorman caught him on the bounce and booted him into the middle of the street. From there the hobo looked back with admiration and exclaimed, "My, what a system!"

In other words, must there not be a value, a good, an end whose intrinsic goodness can motivate a choice before our knowledge of means, conditions, and circumstances will lead us to secure it? Can science possibly justify ideals?

Evil Ideals

It is in this line of thought that the distinction between *de facto* and *de jure* quality becomes clearly necessary. Dewey agrees that there are wrong ideals. Without aesthetic enjoyment mankind might become a race of economic monsters capable of using leisure only in ostentatious display and extravagant dissipation (*Reconstruction in Philosophy,* 127). Apparently no amount of knowledge of interactions and relations will make economic monsters a value. But why not? The peace settlement of World War I was made with the most realistic attention to concrete details of economic advantage, and Dewey never tires of insisting on concrete details. The aims, too, were broadly social and were not limited to private comfort; but at Versailles, according to Dewey, it was attention to economic advantage distributed in proportion to physical power that created future disturbances. And presumably this was bad. The evil of such a situation does not arise from the absence of ideals; much less, it must also be said, from an ignorance of details; but rather the greatest evils arise from the wrong ideals. How, then, can further attention to realistic detail identify valuable ideals? Dewey berates shortsightedness and insists that one should not sacrifice the future to immediate pressure. But will farsightedness solve the problem if it cannot see far enough to pass beyond valuable means to an intrinsically valuable end?

Dewey was aware that this type of refutation would be offered to him. He therefore tried to forestall it by a reference to the Platonic dialogue in which Gorgias praises the art of oratory (*The Quest for Certainty*, 269). Gorgias' brother is a physician, but Gorgias is more successful than his brother in persuading a patient to take the treatment; there are also engineers who lay plans before the city council, but it is Gorgias with his oratory rather than the technicians with their scientific detail who can persuade or dissuade the council. To this eulogy of oratory Plato replies that neither the technician with his knowledge of conditions and interactions, nor the orator with his knack of persuasion, knows whether it is better or worse for the patient to be cured or for the council to be persuaded. A knowledge of ideals, not so derived, is required. Dewey also (*Reconstruction in Philosophy*, 15 ff.) refers to the Platonic illustration that a shoemaker may have scientific knowledge of the construction of shoes, but such knowledge cannot decide whether or not it is good to wear them. But, unfortunately, Dewey does not meet the Platonic position squarely; at least the immediate contexts in the two volumes give no short reply to Plato. One is left, then, to judge the theory as a whole.

That the methods of science cannot be applied in the determination of ethical principles can best be appreciated if one keeps clearly in mind the specific results Dewey thinks he has obtained by his methods. And to make the discussion still more concrete, the ideals mentioned by one of Dewey's wholehearted and influential disciples—Professor William Heard Kilpatrick—will be added to the list. In each case the question must be: Do scientific methods produce these ideals?

The comparison of methods and results is not something that

the humanists can properly complain about. Because of the fundamental position assigned to ethics in this type of philosophy, because of Dewey's complaint that theism and transcendentalism have severed morals from human nature and have destroyed the integrity of both with the environment (*Reconstruction in Philosophy,* Introduction), because opponents of humanism are to be branded as irresponsible social sponges (and, of course, unintelligent obscurantists), and because of the demand that thinking should solve the concrete problems of daily experience, the humanists are under obligation to indicate some detailed guidance. If the methods of science do not in fact establish the ideals they specify, their concrete program fails. And if the empirical methods of the laboratory cannot justify any ideal, the very basis of Dewey's philosophy collapses.

Specifications

In several places Dewey calls for "the directed reconstruction of economic, political and religious institutions" (*The Quest for Certainty,* 259, 282). He wants "the tedium of vacant leisure [to be] filled with images that excite and satisfy" (*Reconstruction in Philosophy,* 103, 127). This, unfortunately, is a little too vague to be classified as an ideal for concrete guidance. It is to be regretted that Dewey is frequently vague. The particular reconstructions of institutions and the particular exciting images must be left vague, for, according to Dewey, reflection ceases to be complete if it is subordinated to maintaining some preconceived purpose. Aiming at a special result is a sign of insincerity. (*Reconstruction in Philosophy,* 145–146).

But if no special reconstruction of society and no particular set of exciting images can be insisted upon, it would seem that the method is of little use in actual situations.

However, Dewey is not always so vague. The special results which are signs of insincerity are chiefly (perhaps always) those of private, one-sided advantage; "a personal end is repulsive" (*Recon-*

struction in Philosophy, 157; compare *Philosophy and Civilization,* 16). An instrumentalist theory of truth, he complains, has too often been thought of in terms of satisfying some purely personal need. This is a mistake. The satisfaction that instrumentalism provides, Dewey explains, is "a satisfaction of the needs and conditions of the problem out of which the idea, the purpose and method of action, arises. It includes public and objective conditions."

Superficially, at least this much may be admitted. Whether I am developing new vaccines or investing in the stock market, there is plenty of stubborn objectivity to be taken into account. And in this sense the problem has "needs and conditions" which must be satisfied. But what shall be said of the prior choice between developing vaccines and investing in the stock market? The former presumably is not privately or personally motivated (though, of course, it may be), and the latter is as good an example as any of purely personal satisfaction. But what procedure of science—either biological science or economic science, not to mention physics and chemistry—demonstrates empirically that a purely private end is repulsive? Certainly there is here an unbridged gap between Dewey's premises and his conclusion, and it would seem that the gap is unbridgeable. Egoism is not so easily refuted.

In addition to the question whether or not science demonstrates the repulsiveness of personal ends, their exclusion still leaves Dewey's position somewhat vague; for even among non-personal, disinterested ends—assuming that such exist—there are incompatible choices. Can science establish one as opposed to another? Where Dewey becomes definite, does he have science for him any more than the opposite choice would have?

For all his general vagueness, there are a few relatively definite ideals that Dewey accepts. He mentions health, wealth, friendship, industry, temperance, courtesy, learning, and initiative (*Reconstruction in Philosophy,* 166–169), as well as lighting, heating, and transportation (*The Quest for Certainty,* 268). These specifications are indeed sufficiently definite; and as they are typical, they go a long way toward rescuing ethics from the bog of eternal values, if not from the rigidity of fixed truths.

Kilpatrick is similarly specific. Bodily health and vigor is a good that no modern-minded man would deny. A well-adjusted personality, satisfying personal relationships, meaningful work as opposed to a life of leisure, music, an adequate social life process, and a non-supernatural religion are examples of Kilpatrick's twelve constituents of the good life. Morality is whatever advances this good life.*

Further specific ideals can be inferred from his depreciation of ancient Sparta's military system and his praise of Periclean Athens (286–289). He is also explicitly opposed to racial discrimination (340), and to high schools with more than 3,000 students (343); he holds that *laissez-faire* is an evil (405), as is also the old-fashioned Americanism that believed in the government's duty to protect private property and to maintain inalienable rights (403, 53–54).

Most emphatically, he is opposed to religious liberty. Not only would he prevent religious groups from maintaining schools and colleges (354), he believes it is "undemocratic" to allow parents to teach the doctrines of their religion to their own children. Apparently he thinks that the government should invade even the home to enforce belief in humanistic secularism. Well, no one can accuse Kilpatrick of being too vague on some points.

Political Implications

That scientific method should generate the ideal of political totalitarianism is a feature of this theory that should be further emphasized. Dewey indicates the connections between science and socialism by pointing out that advances in science and invention depend on the cooperation of many individuals. This leads him to conclude against any selfish and ignoble aims. He repudiates subjectivism and individualism. And to put more force into his theory, he points out that societies exert pressure on recalcitrant individuals. Thus instead of a divine sanction of morality, there is a social sanc-

*William Kilpatrick, *Philosophy of Education,* 97–98, 151–161

tion. Indeed, in an obscurely worded paragraph, Dewey envisages a still greater social compulsion in the future than in the past. Scientists will devise procedures to control the desires of men.

Let Dewey speak for himself:

> It is theoretically conceivable that there should be ethical theory that concerns itself scientifically and objectively with the causal conditions and the concrete consequences of this and that desire. The practical difficulties in the way are immense. Only a slight beginning has been made. But were the enterprise pursued, it would develop, as it matures, techniques for dealing with human nature as we now have them for physical nature. These techniques would not consist in manipulation from without because they would demand cooperative voluntary responses for their realization. Such a science and technique are not conspicuous for their absence (*Problems of Men,* 178–179).

This paragraph with its hope of ascertaining the causes of desire is very cautiously expressed. When at the end he remarks that techniques for controlling men's desires are not conspicuous by their absence, one might suppose that he has only advertising in mind. His repudiation of manipulation from without and his demand for voluntary responses seem to preclude all brutal coercion, all drugs, all Communistic destruction and reconstitution of personality. Yet it is not clear how men's desires can be caused and controlled without any external manipulation at all. Even advertisements are external. To what extent, then, are external devices to be developed? Are they to be applied with or without the victim's consent? It is not inconceivable to cause a desire or voluntary response without the victim's being conscious of the techniques applied to him. At any rate, Dewey has in mind something far different from persuasion and advertisement. And his proposal goes beyond even what he probably had in mind. For, however cautiously one proposes to control men's desires, the stark reality of the theory soon becomes shockingly plain. Dewey wants to manipulate men as completely as science manipulates physical nature. Certain manipulators will control the thoughts of the populace and make everybody desire what the manipulators want them to desire. "Only a slight beginning has been made." The ideal is complete, inescapable control. No longer will it be possible for individuals to want those things they have heretofore wanted. Parents will not be able to want to teach their children their own religion; they will not be able to believe in inalienable rights. As these techniques are developed beyond the inefficient stage to which the Communists have brought them—and this stage is not conspicuous by its absence—propaganda, political regimentation, and brainwashing will banish subjectivism and individualism from ethics, and there will be a thoroughly objective scientific system.

These last few lines are not exactly what Dewey said. What he actually said may be seen in the quoted paragraph or examined in its context in the book. But if this is not what he explicitly said, is it not what the theory means?

There is something else also that Dewey does not say and even seems to deny, but which appears to follow necessarily from his general point of view. This has to do with the role of civil government. In one place Dewey expresses his dislike for an all-powerful state; he also pays his respects to his Vermont ancestors who were neither Communists nor any kind of totalitarians. Such expressions are not to be taken as insincere; yet at the same time his social theory of ethics cannot logically stop short of totalitarianism. If human nature is to be controlled as effectively as physical nature is now controlled, and if the desires of people are to be regulated, onc is forced to ask what agent of social compulsion does the regulating? Where is the focus of the social sanction of morality?

It can hardly be all humanity. Whatever may happen in the future in the way of world government, nations and civilization in the past have been largely separate. And at the present time, there are no demands that are clearly the demands of all humanity. If humanity speaks at all in the babble of the United Nations, it speaks in such an indistinct and ambiguous language that no specific obligation can be discerned. In fact, it is the conflicting demands of different segments of humanity that produce our present international troubles. For the same reason, it is clear that universal society imposes no sanctions. Mankind neither promulgates, imposes, nor enforces any rule. One may rather say, universal society does not exist.

The family is at the other extreme. In numbers it is the smallest society, though in influence and in sanctions it is more effective than humanity at large. Another society is the church, though it goes without saying that Dewey has not based his thinking on any church. Could it then be a group of advertising men or an association of scientists that would control the thoughts of men? If it could be, this group would control the civil officials as well as the other citizens so that this group would either be the government itself or the *Eminence grise* (*ou plutôt rouge*) behind the throne. The society therefore on which instrumentalism must rely, whether Dewey admits it or not, is the nation; for of all societies, the nation can apply the greatest sanctions. But if morality is to be determined by the nation, what else can our duty be but to obey whatever the State commands? Indeed, what else would we be able to desire?

It follows from this that murder and brutality are right whenever the State decides on such a course of action. The State can do no wrong, for right is determined by what the State does.

Disagreement on Murder

Although this totalitarianism seems to be logically implied by Dewey's theory with his condemnation of individualism and his hope of brainwashing the population, yet this is not what Dewey said nor probably what he consciously meant. In one of his books Dewey asserts that no honest person can convince himself that murder would have beneficial consequences, and he also adds that a normal person will immediately resent an act of wanton cruelty (*Ethics,* 265, 292). There are, nonetheless, a large number of people (presumably normal) who enjoy bullfights. But Dewey stakes his claim on normal people who are fair-minded (*Ethics,* 251).

Philosophically, this begs the question. The members of the

S.P.C.A. regard bullfight fans as a low breed of humanity. In return, the latter believe that the former just do not have a normal sense of fun. On what basis then is this disagreement to be resolved? Must not one first define the right and good, and only on this basis decide who is normal and fair-minded? Or can we simply say that these honorific designations are to be applied to the preferences of the majority? The plausibility that a normal person resents wanton cruelty and condemns murder lies in the fact that the statement is true in the United States, at the present time, because of our Christian heritage. But it is not true in Communistic countries. There murder and massacre are definitely accepted as having very beneficial consequences. Now, if Dewey and Kilpatrick succeed in destroying Christianity by prohibiting parents to give their children religious instruction, could anyone be sure that massacre would be still thought wrong? And if a socialistic government learns how to control the desires of most of the population, might it not become true—even in the United States—that every normal, fair-minded person would believe that the torture of political dissenters is a good?*

The reason that Dewey would react violently against such an inference is that he has smuggled viewpoints into his philosophy which either beg the question, or are factually untrue, or are in conflict with his own principles. As has just been indicated, he assumes a universal moral agreement, whether on murder or on bullfights, where none or little exists; and the reader is expected to accept the assumption without question. Dewey's statement about murder and wanton cruelty is not only factually untrue, but it also begs the question because he has nowhere produced scientific evidence that murder never has beneficial results. Nor can his own principles consist with such a fixed moral norm as this would be, if it could be proved. Dewey's insistence on the tentativeness of all

---

*On the degree of Dewey's socialism, see Sidney Hook, *John Dewey,* Chapter XII, and George R. Geiger, *John Dewey in Perspective,* Chapter 8 and the note on page 179.

practical hypotheses requires him to admit that wanton cruelty may some day be the most efficient means to a social goal.

In rejecting personal or private ends, Dewey also assumes that individuals are under an obligation to submit to society. And this society, we have argued, must be the state. But a categorical obligation to obey the state is not a point of universal agreement. Is there then another scientific experiment that could demonstrate this obligation? What if a man says he will be loyal to his family rather than to his nation?

In Russia, of course, they would murder such a person by execution or by working him to death in Siberia, but here we might be inclined to think that the man who disobeys Communism is a moral man and an honorable martyr. The point to be observed is that the various societies, the several nations, and the many families do not agree. They command or recommend quite different types of action. How then is the individual to choose which society he shall obey? If Hitler commands us to massacre the Jews, or if Khrushchev orders us to slaughter the Hungarians, would it be right or wrong to disobey? What theory justifies the supremacy of the State as the judge of right and wrong? What is the basis of any claim that the nation may make on us? Why should we not try to evade the brainwashing of our scientific rulers?

There is another puzzle left by Dewey's theory, though it is not a puzzle that many readers of this book will be called on to solve. But the puzzle is this: How are the rulers to decide what policy to follow? Granted that they can make us desire what they want us to desire, how can they decide what they want us to desire? If morality is the decree of the State, all moral problems are automatically settled for us common slaves. But problems are not automatically settled for the leaders in the Kremlin. They take orders from no one. Science undoubtedly can devise the most effective means to this or that end. But the end is the private preference of the dictator. Dewey may assert that private ends are repulsive, and Kilpatrick may claim that it is undemocratic for parents to teach moral principles to their children, but the claim has not been made good that science can distinguish between *de jure* and *de facto* enjoyments.

Emphasis on disagreements about murder, disagreements between Spanish bullfighters and Puritans, between Kilpatrick and Christian parents, between competing or successive dictators underscore a serious flaw in Dewey's philosophy. He would have to hold, in the latter case, that the dictator would request his scientists to form and control his desires. This is not likely to happen. Or, more broadly, science would have to produce an agreement between parents and educators. In general, Dewey's assumption is that science can produce well nigh universal moral agreement. Or, at the very least, science can determine values. But Dewey has failed the test at its easiest point. Was not murder the clearest example of evil—an example that every fair-minded person would agree to? Yet Dewey has not succeeded in showing how this moral judgment can be justified by scientific procedure. Indeed, for all his insistence that science can solve all problems and that values can only arise through relating means to proximate ends, Dewey, so far as I know, has not given a single instance of thus discovering a value. He seems to admit as much (*The Philosophy of John Dewey,* 592, note). But is it unreasonable to ask for just one instance?

Dewey cannot now respond to the challenge. But we may, by way of illustration, examine how one of his defenders attempts to dispose of the objection that normative principles cannot be deduced from descriptive statements.*

Professor Geiger (109–110) begins by noting that atomic scientists are facing moral problems—"an amoral scientist is not quite a full human being." But this shows only that a man may be both a moralist and a scientist. It is far from showing that values and normative principles can be generated out of scientific descriptive statements. Later (121) he says that most moral questions are not carried back to an ultimate good. This may be a true descriptive statement of how incomplete the thinking of most people is, but a defense of Dewey would require reasons why an appeal to the ultimate is never necessary. Geiger insists on the need of knowing the means to an end, but no reason is given for accepting any end.

*George R. Geiger, *John Dewey in Perspective*

Finally, the author confuses the issue: "Dewey's entire argument stands on the premise that there is no substitute for authenticated knowledge in dealing with problems, wherever those problems may occur" (135). No doubt this is plausible and even true. But it is not to the point. One might as well argue that since there is no substitute for hydrogen in water, it follows that no oxygen is necessary. Let it be granted that a certain amount of "authenticated knowledge" is necessary to accomplish a purpose; let it be granted that a knowledge of means is important; this still gives no help in showing how ends or values can be generated in the manner claimed. When the opponent of Dewey makes the reasonable request to be shown one instance, the substitution of a hopeful appeal to the future for an accomplished success in the past is not satisfactory; it will not do.

The disparity between normative principles and descriptive statements is one of the basic objections to naturalism. Attempts to answer this objection usually, shall we venture to say always, sidestep the issue. To make this evasion more apparent and more embarrassing, one further example will be added.

Is Life Worth Living?

One critic of Dewey remarked that however much instrumentalism asserts universal flux, the system has one eternal, fixed, unchangeable absolute: the value of inquiry, the importance of solving problems. Behind this fixed truth is the more general principle that life is worth living. Surely this point ought not to be evaded and passed over in silence. It has been a matter of disagreement. It marks out an indeterminate situation. It should be a subject of inquiry requiring a solution in terms of some idea that is a plan of action. Nor is it an artificial problem. Many men face it under various forms.

In the twentieth century the form in which death becomes a live option for many materializes under totalitarian oppression. Thousands have risked death by fleeing through the Iron Curtain of barbed wire and machine gun bullets. Other thousands met death in the Hungarian bid for freedom. All of these would doubtless have preferred to live, but by risking death they showed that they thought that life was not worth living under Communism. There is also a smaller number who have committed suicide. Then, too, there are others who have committed suicide without having been driven to it by such oppression. Several of the Stoics decided that it was better to die than live. In the United States also, the suicide rate has risen sharply during the last fifty years. The value of life, therefore, is not an artificial problem, and instrumentalism is obliged to defend its optimistic or at least melioristic attitude. Christianity with its revelational basis asserts that suicide is immoral; but what can be said by an empirical, descriptive philosophy?

This question of suicide is not to be understood as just one detail among many. It is not as though we had canvassed the merits of stealing, lying, adultery, murder, and, oh yes, there is one more, suicide. On the contrary, the mention of suicide is intended to bring to the fore the absolutely indispensable prerequisite of all other ethical decisions. Theft versus honesty and murder versus non-resistance are possible choices only if we have previously decided to continue living. On what basis, therefore, can it be shown that life is worth the time and trouble?

The great majority of modern moralists refuse to face this problem. Kant, to be sure, faced it with both eyes open; but who can judge that his tortured, theoretical solution is other than a complete failure? F.C.S. Schiller, who with James and Dewey is a founder of pragmatic humanism, faced the problem with one eye open. In his volume on *Humanism* he admits that pessimism is a real choice. Indeed it is to his credit that he saw that a pessimist need not hold that there is a surplus of pain over pleasure. If life on the whole is merely boring and dreary, if it has no great and important goals, if it is simply not worth the trouble of going through the motions, then pessimism and possibly suicide are alone rational. But whereas Kant faced this problem squarely, Schiller shortly shuts his one open eye and proceeds as if there were no difficulty. He has no argument against suicide; life for him is merely a personal preference, and for that reason his particular moral choices are merely personal preferences, too.

But the majority of modern ethical and religious writers are not even so open-eyed as Schiller. Both with Dewey and with the others, the usual line of argument proceeds from the false assumption that there is general agreement on moral principles among fair-minded people.

Yet all this that Dewey takes so wholeheartedly for granted has been vigorously denied and attacked by thinkers of world renown and by significant portions of the human race. Buddhism, for instance, holds that pain is a necessary element in the universal process; desire is the cause of pain; and suppression of desire, completed in the unconsciousness of Nirvana, is the only remedy for pain. A Buddhist would probably say that these principles are such obvious conclusions from an observation of the world that only the wilfully blind can fail to see them.

In the western world this view was adopted by Arthur Schopenhauer. True, neither the Buddhists nor Schopenhauer believed that suicide is the proper solution. Nevertheless, it should be clearly kept in mind that the type of life that follows from a pessimistic principle must be vastly different from that based on a confident meliorism.

Or, let us turn from Schopenhauer to Friedrich Nietzsche. Nietzsche was no pessimist; perhaps it is he who might best be called an exuberant optimist. Accepting the universe wholeheartedly, he was impressed by the evolutionary process. In it he saw not merely a struggle for existence, but rather the will to power. Biologists make a fundamental error when they say that the species are important. The existence of species is merely a means for the production of strong individuals. Inherent in the process of life is the tendency to grow and expand, not merely to survive. There are many animal instincts that are positively dangerous to survival, but which are useful in gaining domination. The will to power is not a fiction; it is this world as it really is. And therefore, within the human species, the large numbers of mediocre people are of no importance, and all value is concentrated in the few supermen.

Here two thoughts come to mind. The first, which is of lesser importance, concerns the mediocre multitudes. Since Nietzsche finds value only in the lives of the supermen, there seems no good reason why we ordinary mortals should not end it all. Can I as an individual enter very enthusiastically on an existence whose sole value consists in belonging to a species that might by a sudden mutation produce a superman? What obligation or even advantage have I to take part in this process? Why should I not resign as I resign a lost game of chess?

But a second consideration is more important to the overall argument. According to Nietzsche, the mediocre and weak are immoral. To pity them is a vice. Virtue consists in riding roughshod over the masses and dominating them. Cruelty is the cause of culture. An absolute ruler, like Napoleon, is the acme of happiness. The virtues of Christianity are slavish and degrading. It is unnecessary, however, to expound the details of Nietzsche's morality. The important thing to note is that Schopenhauer, Dewey, and Nietzsche all looked (supposedly) at the same world; but clearly they did not see the same thing. Some see nothing wrong; others see nothing right.

Hence, a first conclusion is inescapable. Those moralists who have proceeded as if all men agree on what is desirable must be judged to have failed. They must be forced to open their eyes and face the basic problems. Not only must they be forced to explain why, instead of brutality and totalitarianism, they prefer certain elements salvaged from Christian morality; they must also be forced to justify life itself. This they have not done, and therefore their systems are failures.

There is also a second conclusion hardly less obvious. All these men, Nietzsche as well as Dewey, seem to think that nature speaks unambiguously. They often write as if an almost casual observation of nature would remove all doubt as to the values they propose. Or—if Dewey insists on a more careful attention to scientific details, particular relationships, manifold causes and conditions—nonetheless the ideal appears automatically. It is as if a list of events could by itself show which events are good and which are bad. But this, I assert, is impossible. No description of the biological or of the historical world suffices for a judgment of evaluation. Napoleon and Pasteur, Jesus and Caesar are equally figures of history. Their deeds can be described to the last detail, but no description can be a criterion for its own moral evaluation.

Concluding Criticism

To return to Dewey's main thesis that science can solve the problem of morality, the criticism that has controlled the argument is two-fold. First, scientific method does not justify the ideals of Dewey and Kilpatrick; and, second, scientific method cannot justify any ideal.

Though the first point is of lesser logical importance, it is not without *ad hominem* value. In addition, it may perhaps find more ready acceptance, for scientists as well as the average citizen can see clearly that there is nothing in laboratory methods that demands as an ideal the governmental suppression of religion.

True, there is a "scientism" adopted by the Communists that holds religion to be an opiate. This atheism would limit all aims and ideals to this world; there is no supernatural realm, no life after death, no future world. And since this is an absolute fixed truth, commissars are justified in preventing parents from teaching religion to their children. But the valid argument that leads from a description of laboratory methods to the conclusion that secularism is desirable does not exist.

Even if it could be shown, as indeed it cannot, that laboratory methods validly imply totalitarian dictatorship, the latter would not thereby become ideal. In such a case many people would choose more freedom and less science. The physical discomforts of a prescientific society are minor in comparison with the spiritual torture of an inquisitorial bureaucracy.

The gap between the premises of scientific method and the ideals which Dewey and Kilpatrick offer as conclusions is no less real, if a trifle less evident, in the case of religious liberty. Good health and speedy transportation have not been made desirable by any increase of scientific technique. They were not in the first place chosen as ideal because of any incipient scientific knowledge. Obviously science has done wonders in medicine and has increased the speed of transportation beyond the imagination even of Jules Verne, but science neither causes men to desire them nor causes them to be desirable. On the contrary, it is because men chose them as ideals that scientists began to look for means of securing them.

Indeed, the more science is stressed as instrumental, the more evident it should be that it cannot establish ends or ideals.

This is the second part of the concluding criticism. Scientific method can produce no ideals whatever. Science is instrumental. If a group of educators wish to extinguish religious liberty, a scientific attention to the details and relationships of psychology, sociology, and politics will help them to their end. The same scientific technique can be used for the opposite purpose. The techniques of medicine can cure diseases that were usually fatal a century ago, but this same technical knowledge can just as easily be used to produce these diseases. In fact, cancer research at present is largely interested in producing cancer. But no instrumental technique, whether medical or political, can furnish any basis for deciding how to use it.

Therefore, the contemporary humanist attempt to solve the problems of ethics by the application of scientific methods must, fortunately, be adjudged a failure. Since, too, this problem—as I have argued elsewhere*—engulfs previous secular theories, such as utilitarianism, it seems to follow that a more sympathetic consideration ought to be given to divine revelation than is customary in the universities of our land.

**A Christian View of Men and Things*, chapter IV

4

Logic

The framework or skeleton on which Dewey's ethics and science are constructed is a theory of logic, or as he frequently prefers to call it, a theory of inquiry. Dewey himself, as well as this monograph, take the term *logic* rather broadly. Deductive logic is but a small part of it; inductive logic or the methods of discovery in science are a larger part; there is also a pragmatic epistemology or instrumentalism and its biological sources as well. The monograph's last main section therefore will be subdivided into Instrumentalism, Behaviorism, and Formal Logic.

Instrumentalism

Dewey never tires of contrasting the ancient ideal of knowledge with his own. The former had some sort of supernatural mind that contemplated changeless being. The realm of opinion and flux was an inferior sphere, hard to relate to the eternal realities. From the disparity between these two worlds spring all the pseudo-problems of traditional philosophy: materialism and idealism, mind and body, appearance and reality, representational ideas and the coherence theory of truth, as well as the possibility of values (*Reconstruction in Philosophy,* 22, 106–112; *Experience and Nature,* 149; *The Quest for Certainty,* 17–25; *Logic, the Theory of Inquiry,* 520 ff.).

To sidestep all these insoluble enigmas, Dewey insists that knowledge does not grasp antecedent reality. Knowledge, as can be seen in its best form—science—looks to the future. It aims at new construction, not at the discovery of the old. Science developed out of ordinary work, because work stimulated people to note and record relationships that might lighten their labor. Thus they invented tools. It is in the process of invention that knowledge is to be found. The immediate qualities of things are disregarded, and traits are sought which are signs of something future. "The very conception of cognitive meaning, intellectual significance, is that things in their immediacy are subordinated to what they portend and give evidence of. . . . The character of intellectual meaning is instrumental." As science improves, the perceived object is eventually stripped of all its immediate qualities, and there is produced an object of knowledge that is an anatomized epitome of just those traits which are of indicative or instrumental import (*Experience and Nature*, 128–129).

Sometimes discovery, historical discovery, is used as evidence that the object of knowledge has been there all the time. We are supposed to uncover it as a treasure hunter finds a buried chest of pirate gold. Thus the Norsemen are said to have discovered America. But did this make America an object of knowledge? Unless the newly found object is used to modify old beliefs, unless it transforms the prior situation, unless it alters the public world in which men publicly act, there is no discovery in any pregnant intellectual sense. That there is an existence antecedent to search and discovery is, of course, admitted (*Philosophy and Civilization*, 54); but it is denied that as such it is an object of knowledge (*Experience and Nature*, 156). The contents of experience are of two distinct types. Some occur with a minimum of foresight and preparation; others are the result of prior intelligent action. Both kinds are *had;* they are enjoyed or suffered; but only the second type, not the first, is known (*The Quest for Certainty*, 243). Or, again, "immediate qualitative experience is not itself cognitive; it fulfils none of the logical conditions of knowledge and of objects *qua* known" (*Logic, the Theory of Inquiry*, 522).

The denial that antecedent being—what is and has been—can be known, however paradoxical it may appear, is defended on the pragmatic or instrumental theory of knowledge. Contrary to the traditional view, knowledge is not a grasp or contemplation of objects given. The Greeks had argued that to know is to know something, something that is, not something that is becoming. That which is becoming is no longer what it was nor is it yet what it will be: The changing is indeterminate and therefore cannot be known. Being is the object of knowledge; knowing, to use Dewey's not altogether accurate characterization, is like taking a snapshot of Being. Contrary to this traditional view, Dewey asserts that knowledge is a mode of practical action; it is "a way of operating upon and with the things of ordinary experience" (*Reconstruction in Philosophy,* 87; *The Quest for Certainty,* 1906). "Thought is not a property of something termed intellect apart from nature; it is a mode of directed overt action" (*The Quest for Certainty,* 166). Reason or intelligence is not a mental substance. It is rather an adverb than a noun; it is a quality of conduct (*Experience and Nature,* 158).

In order better to understand the import of Dewey's assertions, some preliminary analysis and criticism will be of help. If knowledge is a mode of practical action, there must be in the first place something to act on; then comes the action itself; and finally a new object is constructed. The preceding phrases seem to locate knowledge in the second of these three terms and seem to deny that the other two can be known. Rather obviously Dewey holds that the first cannot be known. He has constantly repeated that there is no knowledge of antecedent being. But if so, how could he consistently assert that there is an existence antecedent to search and discovery? If it is not an object of knowledge (*Experience and Nature,* 156), how does he know that there is such an existence? Dewey admits that the "given" is a pervasive quality so undetermined that it can be called only a blooming, buzzing confusion (*Philosophy and Civilization,* 105, 107). Is this concept of an unknowable existence legitimate? Kant had some difficulty along this line, and one hardly expects to find it reappearing in Dewey. The non-philosophical scientist would ordinarily think that he could know, before experimentation, that the object was black, wet, heavy, or sweet. This type of knowledge would never satisfy Plato's standards for the world of Ideas, but is it not necessary to and well within the range of Dewey's more tentative and changing knowledge?

It is difficult to imagine how Dewey's system could get started without this type of knowledge. Yet Dewey is reluctant to admit that experience of black, wet, and heavy is knowledge, whether that experience comes at the beginning of the scientific process or at the end. Science or knowledge produces wet water for non-cognitive enjoyment. Knowledge seems to take place between the first casual enjoyment and the final enjoyment secured by scientific control. But the two extremes are non-cognitive. This aspect of Dewey's thought should be carefully considered. Is there such a thing as a non-cognitive experience? Can we enjoy the wetness of water in quenching thirst without knowing that it is wet and cool? If one wishes arbitrarily to restrict the term *knowledge* to the scientific procedure of controlling the water supply, one may indeed give a good account of such control; but such a restriction will prevent the formulation of a satisfactory general theory of knowledge. It is hard to avoid the impression that Dewey offers us a narrow view and asks us to accept it as completely general.

The manner in which Dewey substitutes constructed objects of knowledge for the immediate qualities leads to further difficulties. When in many places he speaks of selecting relationships rather than qualities as the material for scientific inquiry, when he speaks of "noting and recording of nature's doings," and when he subjects "thought to a pertinent order of space and time" (*Experience and Nature,* 121), are we to suppose that these doings and this order are solely our muscular manipulations of things, our overt action, and not something that was "there" before we acted? Can we sharply distinguish between qualities and relationships in such a way that the former cannot and the latter can be known (*Experience and Nature,* 129; *Philosophy and Civilization,* 93)? If critics of Aristotle find it difficult to maintain the distinctness of his categories of quality and relation, one might suspect that Dewey, with his distaste for Aristotle, would be even less successful. But in any case, if relations are the proper objects of science, and if our overt action modifies "qualities in such ways that *relations* become manifest" (*The Quest for Certainty,* 104), it is hard to identify our overt action with these relations. In other words, if knowledge is our way of operating on things, can relations, which result from but which are not our actions, be noted, recorded, and known? This question becomes all the more difficult when Dewey distinguishes between temporal events (of which our manipulations must be examples) and the abstract, non-temporal, and, if you will, eternal relations (*Experience and Nature,* 148).

Just above, the knowledge situation was divided into antecedent existence, our planning and action, and the end product. The analysis has carried us from the antecedent existence to the end product. In consistency, so it would seem, Dewey ought to deny that this last is an object of knowledge. But here he is more hesitant than before. Many times he denies a knowledge of antecedent being, but in some instances he allows a knowledge of subsequent being:

> Since every special case of knowledge is constituted as the outcome of some special inquiry, the conception of knowledge as such can only be a generalization of the properties discovered to belong to conclusions which are outcomes of inquiry. Knowledge, as an abstract term, is a name for the product of competent inquiries" (*Logic, the Theory of Inquiry,* 8).

What then is the case? Is knowledge to include the antecedent material which is the point of departure, the overt process, and the product as well? Is it to be restricted to the product alone as this quotation seems to say? Or is knowledge to be equated with the overt behavior? There seems to be a real difficulty here. The more Dewey insists that ideas are plans of action, the less can he admit that either antecedent existence or subsequent products are objects of knowledge. It is necessary, therefore, to see what Dewey has to say about ideas, for surely ideas play an important part in knowing.

All the traditional philosophies—not only ancient but modern as well—consider ideas to be in some way representative of antecedent reality. Sensational empiricism most obviously denies that thought is originative. Originative thought would be error. Idealism, even though it rejects the so-called representational theory of truth, makes the same denial. Whatever creative activity is allowed to a productive imagination or a faculty of synthesis, this action is entirely mental and concrete appearances remain obdurate. In contrast, Dewey proposes to begin by supposing that all we know about ideas is derived from their role in experimental procedure (*The Quest for Certainty,* 110). In science, of course, this is operationalism, as previously explained. Here Dewey applies the principle more generally, or, we might better say, assimilates all thinking to the processes of science. After a detailed explanation of this supposition, Dewey concludes, "Ideas are statements, not of what is or has been, but of acts to be performed" (*The Quest for Certainty,* 138; *Philosophy and Civilization,* 25). For example: To judge that candy is sweet, without at the moment tasting it, is to predict that when it is tasted a sweet sensation will occur.

> Similarly, to think of the world in terms of mathematical formulae of space, time, and motion is not to have a picture of the independent and fixed essence of the universe. It is to describe experienceable objects as material upon which certain operations are performed (*The Quest for Certainty,* 137; *Philosophy and Civilization,* 106).

This last sentence renews the difficulty mentioned shortly above. If we describe objects, even for the purpose of performing certain operations upon them, have we not an idea of antecedent being that is not a plan of action? Dewey does not help himself too much by adding, "Knowledge which is merely a reduplication of what exists already in the world may afford us the satisfaction of a photograph, but that is all" (*The Quest for Certainty,* 137). In this sentence he seems to admit a representative knowledge of antecedent existence. Whether or not the satisfaction it gives is of little value, the main question must be pressed: Is it knowledge and is it an idea? If it is, Dewey's other phrases are undermined; indeed, his whole philosophy is overturned; therefore, no doubt, he is here speaking only by way of accommodation and *ad hominem*. It must be accommodation, for after saying (as previously quoted) that thought is directed overt action, he continues, "Ideas are anticipatory plans and designs which take effect in concrete reconstruction of antecedent conditions of existence" (*The Quest for Certainty,* 166–167; *Reconstruction in Philosophy,* 144; *Philosophy and Civilization,* 31).

The same view is expressed in many other passages. A favorite description is that ideas are tools, whose "value resides not in themselves but in their capacity to work" (*Reconstruction in Philosophy,* 145). Concepts and theories "are instrumental to an active reorganization of the given environment" (*Reconstruction in Philosophy,* 156). Now, a physical tool is not identical with the user's overt actions; but if these idea-tools are habits or reactions of an organism, the designation of an idea as a tool still leaves us within the limits of behavior. Thus, "a thing is more significantly what it makes possible than what it immediately is." That is to say, although in some dubious sense we may perhaps "know" an antecedent thing, our significant idea of the thing is its productive work. To continue the quotation:

> The very conception of cognitive meaning, intellectual significance, is that things in their immediacy are subordinated to what they portend and give evidence of. . . . The character of intellectual meaning is instrumental (*Experience and Nature,* 128).

One of Dewey's clearest statements as to the reference of concepts is found in an earlier essay in which he charges William James with ambiguity. A summary of half a dozen pages will be most enlightening (*Essays in Experimental Logic,* 312–316). James had said that the function of philosophy is to discover what definite difference a world-formula will make in our life, if this one rather than another be true. Dewey objects that this form of the question assumes the meaning of the world-formula as given, whereas the function of philosophy should be to clarify the meaning of the formula taken as a program of behavior for modifying the existing world. He therefore asks,

> Does Mr. James employ the pragmatic method to discover the value in terms of consequences in life of some formula which has its logical content already fixed; or does he employ it to criticize and revise and, ultimately, to constitute the meaning of that formula?

Dewey repeats this double question in several forms. Does the idea of a providential God, if true, justify confidence in the future, or does the concept of confidence in the future define and replace earlier notions of God? Is the pragmatic test supposed to superadd a value to a meaning already fixed, or does it constitute the entire meaning of the terms? "For myself," Dewey concludes, "I have no hesitation in saying that it seems unpragmatic for pragmatism to content itself with finding out the value of a conception whose own inherent significance pragmatism has not first determined." Thus the previous point is corroborated: Knowledge is not concerned "with disclosure of the characteristics of antecedent existences and essences" (*The Quest for Certainty,* 71).

Incidentally, this leaves Dewey without justification for quoting and misinterpreting the Gospel statement, "By their fruits ye shall know them" (*Reconstruction in Philosophy,* 156).

Before the criticism concerning the identity of the object of knowledge is further developed, one additional phase of Dewey's view needs mention. If knowledge or experimentation produces the objects that have the quality of being known—that is, if knowing is literally and physically constructive, or reconstructive, and not merely representative—it is most plausible to say that antecedent nature is "inherently indeterminate or doubtful" and that thinking transforms the problematic situation into one relatively settled and clear (*The Quest for Certainty,* 227). If doubt were merely a subjective feeling of uncertainty, to be banished by a feeling of assurance, thinking would cease to be an effort to change the objective situation. We must recognize "the objective character of indeterminateness: it is a real property of some natural existences" (*The Quest for Certainty,* 231). Also, in the last few pages of his discussion of freedom (*Human Nature and Conduct,* Chapter IV, section 3), Dewey wants "possibilities open in the *world,* not in the will."

The objective character of indeterminateness is particularly important for logic. Dewey defines inquiry as the controlled transformation of an indeterminate situation into a determinate one. This doubtfulness is not a mental affair. It is the *situation* that has these traits.

> *We* are doubtful because the situation is inherently doubtful. . . . consequently, situations that are disturbed and troubled, confused or obscure, cannot be straightened out, cleared up and put to order, by manipulation of our personal states of mind. . . . The habit of disposing of the doubtful as if it belonged only *to us* rather than to the existential situation . . . is an inheritance from subjectivistic psychology. . . . It is, accordingly, a mistake to suppose that a situation is doubtful only in a "subjective" sense (*Logic, the Theory of Inquiry,* 105–106, 161).

In the following chapter, Dewey uses a case at civil or criminal law as an illustration of doubtful situations. And finally, "the ultimate end and test of all inquiry is the transformation of a problematic situation (which involves confusion and conflict) into a unified one" (*Logic, the Theory of Inquiry,* 491).

Now, for a few moments, let us consider whether it is plausible to regard antecedent being—about which we know so little or even nothing at all—as inherently indeterminate. One can agree that "personal states of doubt that are not evoked by and are not relative to some existential situation are pathological" (*Logic, the Theory of Inquiry,* 106), without coming to an indeterministic conclusion. Take as an example any chess problem in which white is to move and mate in three. In this case, is not every one of Dewey's assertions falsified? The "situation," apart from our minds, is not inherently indeterminate. Its factors are all fixed and only one solution is possible. The doubt, therefore, is solely in the mind; *we* are doubtful, perhaps in spite of it, but surely not because the situation is doubtful. The situation in itself is already a unified one and needs no transformation—it is not even necessary to move the pieces overtly.

This example of chess also points up the difference between two inquirers. For one, the problem is exceedingly difficult; for the other, it is easy or perhaps already solved. The problem is the same situation, if we separate the situation from the inquirer's state of mind as Dewey has so sharply done. Consequently, the doubt, the disturbance, the obscurity belongs only to the inquirer, whether or not this is an inheritance from subjective psychology.

In spite of himself, so it would seem, Dewey fails to avoid this subjectivism. A situation is confused, he says, if "its outcome cannot be anticipated"; it is obscure when its "consequences cannot be easily made out"; it is conflicting "when it tends to evoke discordant responses" (*Logic, the Theory of Inquiry,* 106). But in the terms *anticipated, clearly made out,* and *evoked responses,* it is hinted that the indeterminacy of the situation depends on the inquirer's state of mind. All too often, one is forced to conclude, Dewey smuggles into his account elements that he explicitly denies. This has been seen above and will again be seen below.

We shall not permit Dewey to dismiss chess as a trivial game and to assert that it is not an example of thinking. A restriction of thinking to some particular form of thinking might lead to valuable discoveries about that particular form, but it would also have to be recognized that a narrow theory cannot be substituted for a general explanation. The example of chess, therefore, is pertinent. However, chemistry should also be considered.

Chemistry, or physics, is more complicated than chess, and the overt actions of experimentation are necessary to resolve our doubts. Yet this does not necessarily imply that the external situation itself is indeterminate. Possibly, previous scientists have been mistaken on the point, but it has seemed plausible to suppose that the characteristics of elements were fixed and that their compounds occurred deterministically. Even when scientific law came more recently to be regarded as statistical, some scientists continued to believe that the ultimate particles are not inherently indeterministic. Now, an experimental and logically compelling proof of determinism is not to be had. It is not by any such method that Dewey can be once and for all refuted. But there is a twist to the argument that does not much favor Dewey's assertion that situations are inherently undetermined.

Ideas, it has been seen, are tools; their intellectual content is found in the actions they direct. God, if the term means anything at all, is certain aspects of our behavior. Well then, the idea of an inherently indeterminate situation is itself a plan of action, and its content too is found in subsequent situations. Just what actions the idea of determinism means and what different actions indeterminism means may be interesting questions. Does the former mean a confident procedure and the latter a hesitant procedure? If this seems farfetched, perhaps they are not plans of action and therefore not ideas at all. But if Dewey's theory of an indeterminate situation is an idea, it cannot be a description of an antecedent state of affairs. All ideas are forward looking; they do not state what is or has been; therefore, "an indeterminate situation" must mean something that will occur in the future. It cannot be a *terminus a quo* that exists before the inquiry begins. Hence Dewey's theory of inquiry makes its own starting point unknowable.

The impossibility of knowing the past comes to a focus in the study of history. If the content of ideas consists in future actions, can it be known that Columbus discovered America or that Caesar fought in Gaul? In the *Journal of Philosophy,* Volumes XIX and XXI, Dewey argued this point with other contributors. The distinguished Professor Blanshard analyzes this discussion.*

Various phrases, such as "ideas are intentions to act," by which Dewey stresses the forward-looking nature of philosophy, led Pro-

*Brand Blanshard, *The Nature of Thought,* 359ff. The remainder of Blanshard's chapter also, to which so few exceptions can be taken, is a necessity for serious students of Instrumentalism. In addition, Bertrand Russell, in *The Philosophy of John Dewey,* edited by Paul Arthur Schilpp, makes highly important criticisms. The present monograph, so far as is possible, attempts to avoid repeating what has already been so well stated. Of course, some repetition (at least specification) of the more comprehensive objections cannot be avoided.

fessor Blanshard to conclude that no thought can mean or refer to the past. "In judgments about the past," Dewey had said, "the nature of the past event is subject-matter required in order to make a reasonable judgment about the future. The latter thus constitutes the object or genuine meaning of the judgment" (Blanshard, 359). But this conclusion, in which Professor Blanshard was not alone, Dewey repudiated in the articles mentioned. Every judgment, to be sure, refers to the future, but some judgments may also refer to the past.

Dewey explains it as follows: Judgment about a past event, like every other kind of judgment, is a process of settling a doubt. Now, in every inquiry there are two distinct factors. First, there is a "subject-matter," a great mass of accepted facts and considerations which are taken for granted and are used as a basis for reaching a solution. Then, second, there is the "reference," the "object," or the "meaning" of the inquiry, which will be expressed in the verdict. The former provides the retrospective reference; the latter is the inquiry's main concern.

Although this debate begun in the *Journal* started a long time ago, it still continues, and Professor Blanshard is not the only one who calls into question Dewey's knowledge of past events. Much later, in the Schilpp volume, Professor Arthur E. Murphy faces the same difficulty, and it is worthwhile to note Dewey's reply.

> Mr. Murphy is not alone in being troubled by my denial that antecedent conditions constitute the objects of knowledge. *If* I have written anything affirming that antecedent objects are not capable of being known and are not as matter of fact known, *if,* in Mr. Murphy's language, I have asserted their "inaccessibility," any one, myself included, ought to be troubled. . . . Instead of denying that unperceived antecedent conditions are objectives of knowledge in the first context, I have very explicitly stated that no problem as to existential matters can be resolved except by inquiries which *ascertain antecedent conditions not previously observed* (*The Philosophy of John Dewey,* 565).

Dewey then continues by saying that these antecedent objects are not the complete and final object of knowledge and do not satisfy the conditions of a *generalized* theory of knowledge because knowledge also and mainly has a future reference.

One must therefore ask how it is that critics of Dewey return to this point which he claims to have explained so very explicitly. Are the critics merely inattentive or perhaps a little dull? Or, could it be that Dewey's answers to their criticisms seem inadequate? Is Dewey here relying on some common sense view to which his precise theory does not entitle him? Certainly Professor Blanshard had not failed to see Dewey's alleged distinction between antecedent subject matter and the future reference of judgment. His criticism does not arise because of inattention, but because his close attention convinces him that this distinction cannot fit into Dewey's theory.

Professor Blanshard attempts to apply this distinction to the historical assertion that Swift married Stella. The subject-matter on which this biographical conclusion rests is all the accepted evidence. What then is the object or meaning of the conclusion? One would expect that this meaning would be future consequences, plans of action, anticipations of things still to come. But Dewey says that the object is more complicated than this. The meaning of an historical judgment is the entire continuum of events stretching from the past even on to present and future consequences. "The past by itself and the present by itself are both arbitrary selections which mutilate the complete object of judgment."

Though this interpretation of historical judgments is ingenious and plausible, Professor Blanshard regards it as untenable. The past event cannot be identified either as subject-matter or as meaning. If it were subject-matter, the assertion Swift married Stella would be a fact taken for granted on the basis of which some other judgment would be inferred. But it is the assertion itself that is the point of the inquiry. It is precisely what is not taken for granted. On the other hand, the assertion cannot be identified as meaning either. The past event surely cannot be the temporal continuum of past, present, and future. On this point, Professor Lovejoy had made the incisive comment that Dewey, when he shows a retrospective judgment to contain an implicit reference to the future, believes he is relieved of all logical concern about the primary reference to the past. The chief contention of instrumentalism is that thought is an organic adjustment to get something done. The theory demands exclusion of references to the past, and Dewey's attempt to make history plausible is an unassimilated afterthought. Historical inquiry (whatever practical end it may also have) is palpably not, in its central assertions, concerned with action or control at all, or with any future consequences whatever.

After the exchange of articles in the *Journal of Philosophy,* Dewey returned to the discussion of history in *Logic* (230–239). Instead of facing the main criticism squarely, he begins by asking:

> Given temporal continuity, what is the relation of propositions about an extensive past durational sequence to propositions about the present and future? Can the historical continuum involved in admittedly historical propositions of the past be located in the past or does it reach out and include the present and future?

This seems to be an inauspicious formulation, if the knowledge of a past event is to be justified. Lovejoy's criticism applies in full force. The formulation soon shifts to a question of what present evidence makes some judgments about the past more credible than others. Then follow some nine pages of elementary historiography. Not only does he note the type of evidence and the necessity of inference, which an uneducated reader of history might be unaware of; he also shows the prevalence of value judgments, adopted from the culture of the historian, which lead to the rewriting of the history in a later century. In other words, a history book depends on selecting material, and selection is guided by what one thinks important. Toward the end of the section Dewey concludes,

> Our entire discussion of historical determinations has disclosed the inadequacy and superficiality of the notion that since the past is its immediate and obvious object, therefore the past is its

> exclusive and complete object (*Logic, the Theory of Inquiry,* 237).

It is not clear that even this conclusion is entirely justified. There is a sense in which the "object" of inquiry is entirely whether or not Swift married Stella. But aside from this the main criticism remains that instrumentalism provides for no ideas of past events. Dewey may and does give a good account of historiography, but what was required and what he avoided was an explanation of how a knowledge of the past is consistent with his theory of ideas.

Before leaving these criticisms of instrumentalism by Blanshard and Lovejoy, we must return to another phase of the interchange between Dewey and Murphy. Substituting infantile paralysis and the batting average of the New York Yankees for Swift and Stella, Murphy claims that Dewey cannot allow knowledge of the past, although most inquiry aims at finding out just such antecedent existences. Naturally, to prepare for his criticisms, Professor Murphy briefly characterizes Dewey's position, both by quotations and summaries.

Dewey in his reply (*The Philosophy of John Dewey,* 557–558) quotes two of these summaries. First,

> [Dewey's theory of inquiry] refers us instead to a theory about the role of ideas as instruments to be used in so altering a present indeterminate situation that an enjoyed future experience, itself non-cognitive but worthwhile on its own account, will reliably ensue, through the use of procedures which have proved their instrumental value in this capacity.

Now, so it seems to me, this characterization of Dewey's view is about as good as can be made in so few lines. And we must remember that it occurs in the context of a long article that fixes its meaning. Furthermore, it seemed to me that Murphy as well as Blanshard had touched upon a vital flaw in Dewey's philosophy. But to my dismay, as I read down the page, Dewey disposed of all our criticisms by saying, "I am so far from recognizing my theory of inquiry in the report Dr. Murphy makes of it, that, as presented, it seems to me quite as unintelligible as it does to Mr. Murphy."

It need hardly be mentioned that Dewey would be as little able to recognize his theory in this study as in Murphy's and Blanshard's. Since he is now dead, the reader is left alone to decide whether Dewey meant what his critics say or whether he meant something totally different—so poorly expressed that everyone else has misunderstood it.

Dewey quotes Professor Murphy a second time:

> We have already seen [presumably in the passages quoted] he regards it [knowing] as a use of ideas as signs of possible future experiences and means for effecting the transition to such experiences in a satisfactory manner. These future experiences, insofar as they terminate inquiry, will not be cases of "knowing," that is, of the use of given experiences as signs of something else.

Here, unfortunately, Murphy called an idea a sign instead of a plan for future action. Dewey belabors him on this. Ideas are not signs. "Signifying capacity belongs *only* to observed facts or data" (*The Philosophy of John Dewey*, 558). But since Murphy also said that ideas were *means* for effecting the transition to the desired situation, one still wonders that Dewey can reply, "I regret my inability to identify any part [!] of my theory in the above passages." Dewey then restates his theory. "What I have said is that ideas are correlated, in strictly conjugate fashion, with discriminated material of observation, the former serving to indicate a possible mode of operative solution and the latter serving to locate and delimit a problem, so that a resolved situation is attained (if it *is* attained) by the operational interaction with each other of observed and ideational contents." But though Dewey's restatement is slightly fuller than Murphy's brief characterization, the main difference is only that Dewey is more pedantic. If ideas are *correlated* with discriminated material of observation, then the idea *is* not the discrimination. But how can one discriminate without ideas? How can material of observation itself locate and delimit a problem? The main objection therefore still stands, unless perchance behaviorism can answer these questions.

Behaviorism

Although behaviorism might not seem to be properly classified under the heading of logic—for it claims to be science, psychology, and biology—yet Dewey connects it so strictly with epistemology that this is where it must be considered. For Dewey, one might say, knowledge is a subdivision of biology. References to two of his works are sufficient.

The chapter, "Habits and Will," stresses habits and insists that action must precede thought. Habits form ideas. A "will" to do good is defeated by bad habits.

> In the case of no other engine does one suppose that a defective machine will turn out good goods simply because it is invited to. . . . Refusal to recognize this fact only leads to a separation of mind from body, and to supposing that mental or "psychical" mechanisms are different in kind from those of bodily operations and independent of them (*Human Nature and Conduct,* Chapter I, section ii; compare *The Quest for Certainty,* 123, 149–150).

To be noted in this quotation is Dewey's comparison of the mind with an engine and his more literal assertion that mental mechanisms do not differ in kind from bodily operations.

Later, the same view is repeated more emphatically:

> Habits formed in the process of exercising biological aptitudes are the sole agents of observation, recollection, foresight and judgment: a mind or consciousness or soul in general which performs these operations is a myth . . . . Knowledge which is not projected against the black unknown lives in the muscles,

> not in consciousness (*Human Nature and Conduct,* Chapter III, section i; compare *Logic, the Theory of Inquiry,* vi; *The Quest for Certainty,* 86, 166).

There is, however, a difference between Dewey's behaviorism and certain other varieties. Although this distinction is found in the earlier work, Dewey was called upon to repeat it later. For the purpose of this monograph the distinction is unimportant, but the reiteration of naturalism shows that the earlier passages have not been misinterpreted. In answer to various objections Dewey wrote,

> Although the psychological theory involved is a form of behaviorism . . . behavior is not viewed as something taking place in the nervous system or under the skin of an organism, but always, directly or indirectly, in obvious overtness or at a distance through a number of intervening links, an interaction with environing conditions (*The Philosophy of John Dewey,* 555).

This is indeed what he had already said: "Habits incorporate an environment within themselves. They are adjustments *of* the environment, not merely *to* it" (*Human Nature and Conduct,* Chapter I, section iii). To the same effect is his reply to Parodi. A quality such as red, says Dewey, occurs like any other natural event, whether within an organism or outside one:

> There is no passage from the physical to the mental, from an external world to something felt. . . . When, however, a quality is termed a "sensation" . . . it is now placed in a specially selected connection, that to the organism or self. Pending the outcome of an inquiry not yet completed, one may not know whether a quality, say red, belongs to *this* or *that* object in the environment, nor indeed whether it may not be the product of intra-organic processes as in the case of "seeing stars" after a blow on the head. In other words, the occurrence of qualities upon my view is a purely natural event (*The Philosophy of John Dewey,* 599).

This attempt to account for *sensation* by attaching the quality red to an organism instead of to a barn draws attention to a great deal of vagueness and ambiguity. One wishes to know how an organism has a quality and how a barn has a quality. If there is any difference in the having, if a sensation is to be distinguished from a coat of paint, the difference is obscured by the indiscriminate use of the verb *have*. In one place he says, "the object of thought, designated propositionally, is a quality that is first directly and unreflectively experienced or had" (*Philosophy and Civilization,* 107). In another place he says, "A particular painting [is said] to have a Titian or Rembrandt quality. . . . It is not anything that can be expressed in words, for it is something that must be *had*" (*Logic, the Theory of Inquiry,* 70). Does the word *had* mean the same thing in these two cases? If a painting *has* a quality in one sense, and I *have* a quality in another sense, and if—as behaviorism holds—this second having is not a mental or felt having, but is a natural or what for the moment we shall call a physico-chemical event, it becomes imperative to distinguish these two in precise detail. It is most unfortunate to confuse them in a single form of expression. The reduction of sensation to a physico-chemical event will be discussed a few paragraphs below when the force of some of these remarks will become more evident. But at the moment one can only be confused by Dewey's language. He says, "There are two dimensions of experienced things: one that of having them, and the other of knowing about them" (*Experience and Nature,* 21). And again, "Complex and active animals *have* feelings which vary abundantly in quality. . . . They *have* them, but they do not know they have them" (*Experience and Nature,* 258). The implausibility of this becomes evident when any one of us *has* a toothache. The point is that Dewey faces a dilemma. He wants both scientific behaviorism with its denial of anything mental, and he also wants feelings and sensations. The best way to include both in one theory is by the use of vague, ambiguous terminology.

Dewey's behaviorism, and no doubt all forms of behaviorism, acquire whatever plausibility they may seem to possess because of two interacting factors. The first of these is the boast of scientific methodology. This suffices to becloud the initial implausibility that I am no more conscious of a sensation of red, a mental or "felt" awareness, than a barn is conscious of its red paint. The second factor is the behaviorist's trick of smuggling in all the advantages of consciousness after having denied its existence.

When Dewey objects to Russell's remarks on the privacy and subjectivity of perception, he insists that one's perception of the sun is merely a more complex event than the shining of the sun itself. The fact that perception occurs in the retina does not make it private, though it may make it more difficult to observe. And "as for the argument that experience is private because no two persons have exactly the same experience, I suppose it is true that exactly the same physical event does not occur twice" (*Problems of Men,* 177). Perceptions then may be individual, as events in two test tubes are; but a perception is no more mental or private than the paint on the barn. The difference between the latter and the former, aside from being more complex, was said to consist in "a specially selected connection, that to the organism or self." This is the point at which a major part of the smuggling occurs.

Organism is one of the terms in which many of the difficulties are hidden. What precisely is the difference between the shining of the sun and the organism which in connection with the sun provides for the natural occurrence of a sensation? The assertion of the behaviorist is that organisms, which in the last repeated quotation Dewey merged with the *self,* do not differ in kind from any other bodies. A person or self, therefore, is essentially similar to an engine, a machine, or a test tube. Mental mechanisms are no different in kind from bodily operations. Knowledge lives in the muscles, and biological functions—formed into habits—are the sole agents of recollection and foresight. But, although such are the behaviorists' assertions, no scientific evidence or explanation is forthcoming. The vague mention of a "specially selected connection" contrasts strongly with a scientific description in blueprint detail of any engine or machine. No explanation is offered to render plausible the possibility of an engine's recollecting or exercising foresight.

Organism is not the only undefined term. Dewey avoids facing problems squarely by use of the term *habit* also. What is a habit? How is a habit formed? What can be meant by saying that habits are "adjustments *of* the environment, not merely *to* it"?

Here the discussion takes two directions. First, the account tends to erase the distinction between organism and environment. Habit is an adjustment of the environment; and since habits are the sole agents of observation, it follows that the environment as well as the organism observes and recollects. Behavior, so Dewey said—and behavior must include knowing—does not take place under the skin of an organism, but always in obvious overtness or at a distance. Now, in Dewey's pedantic reply to Murphy, he insists (because of excusable omission in Murphy's brief summary) that there be operational interaction between observed and ideational contents. If, however, the environment does as much observing as the organism does, what becomes of the assumed distinctions between observed material and ideational factors?

The second line of discussion relative to habit returns to its definition. What is a habit? There is one passage in which Dewey seems to give a formal definition of *habit*. Speaking of a circuit whose first phase is the tension of various elements of organic energy and whose second phase is the institution of integrated interaction of organism and environment, he says, "A certain modification of environment has also occurred. . . . On the other hand, there is change in the organic structures that conditions further behavior. This modification is termed habit" (*Logic, the Theory of Inquiry*, 31). And on the next page he tells us that repetition does not play the role popularly assigned to it, but that habits are tightened up "by the institution of effective integrated interaction of organic-environing energies." This last phrase expresses no definite meaning. Neither does the whole passage. Since every physiological event in some way conditions future behavior, a chemical change in the blood stream can qualify under this definition—but not only in the blood stream, nor merely under the skin; consider any event in the environment: The chemical reaction of one element with another is an adjustment of, as well as to, the environment. At least the sulphur adjusts to the hydrogen and both adjust to the oxygen. But shall we call H_2SO_4 a habit? If such a chemical reaction is a habit, have not all habits, in a naturalistic philosophy, been reduced to chemical reactions? If, however, this is not so, what is the difference between a chemical reaction and a habit? It is hard to find answers to such questions in Dewey's texts. His use of terms such as *organism, habit,* and *sensation* is entirely inadequate and is particularly inappropriate for those whose main boast is in scientific methodology.

The reference above to reducing habit and sensation to a chemical reaction leads on to another phase of the same difficulty, for under such ambiguity there is more smuggled in than can be brought to light in a few lines. If an idealist charges behaviorism with being materialistic, there comes an indignant denial of atomism and reductionism. Hard pellets moving in space is no longer a suitable picture of the universe, and the behaviorist has no desire to make knowledge "nothing but" the motion of particles. Instead, he gaily identifies reality with the physical universe in all its complexity. Reality is nature. But precisely here is the trouble. The physical universe is left undefined and nature unexplained. Nature cannot be atoms, for atoms are plans of future human action and not a description of antecedent being. But if nature is not atoms in motion, what is it? Dewey, as we have seen before, is extremely vague about the original existence. Yet, to judge the assertion that the human mind can grow out of nature, one would have to know what the nature of nature is. If reductionism is to be justly repudiated, the behaviorist is obliged both to characterize physical reality and to show in detail how it produces habits, recollection, and foresight. Dewey does none of this. The term *nature* is left vague and empty, or, at most, natural is contrasted with the supernatural. But the supernatural, so excluded from reality, is not only God, it is also the conscious mind. If, furthermore, the behaviorist becomes a little religious, as humanism sometimes finds it polite to be, nature even takes on some of the attributes of God. And the inconsistency of this unwitting acknowledgment of something beyond naturalism can be disguised only by means of pervasive ambiguity.

A comprehensive analysis of behaviorism will not be undertaken here. Some further psychological objections are forcefully stated in a work previously recommended, namely, *The Nature of Thought,* by Brand Blanshard, volume I, chapter ix. However, because of Dewey's main interests, it is pertinent and imperative at least to mention the relation between behaviorism and values.

Dewey, of course, is tremendously interested in values. One of his boasts is that he has rescued values from the dark dead world of Newtonian science. Yet one wonders whether behaviorism can offer anything less dark and dead. Is this not another instance of Dewey's claiming values to which his philosophy does not entitle him?

If, for example, a sensation is merely a more complex event than the shining of the sun, and yet of the same kind, how could it have more value or any value? Is complexity *ipso facto* valuable? An earthquake in an uninhabited region is more complex than the simple motion of a single particle, but neither seems to have any value in itself. They are both physical events. One is larger than the other, but that is all that can be said.

No doubt two different events lead to two different results. In his discussions of value, Dewey places great emphasis on means and results. The former are to be judged by the latter. But if the two results are equally physical events, the original question reappears. A result which in itself has no value cannot confer value on its means.

Only as affecting an organism, particularly a human organism, can the shining of the sun or the occurrence of an earthquake be said to have value or disvalue. This returns us once more to the ambiguity of the term *organism.*

If the functioning of an organism is of the same kind as—although much more complicated than—most physico-chemical processes, if pain is not mentally felt nor pleasure enjoyed, if red on the retina is the same as red on the barn and there is no red in the mind, then—with all other values—the value of this discussion vanishes. The functioning of Dewey's organism and environment, and the functioning of my organism and environment—in spite of the non-behavioristic intellectual incompatibility—are equally natural events. In him biological aptitudes developed in one direction; in me different habits grew. There is, however, no felt difference, for nothing is mental or felt. Only a non-behaviorist looking from the outside on Dewey's world could recognize the differences of natural complexity. This non-behavioristic soul would see that the biology of my organism—i.e., the arguments I have here adduced—are just as natural, just as good, and just as valuable as Dewey's. Or, more properly, this non-behavioristic soul would see that the publications of Dewey were just as natural, just as valueless, just as meaningless as the motion of a particle. If some of Descartes' disciples, as is reported, deliberately tortured animals to show their sincerity in holding to Cartesian automatism, could we expect a sincere behaviorist to feel compunction against torturing human beings in order to achieve his political ambitions?

The smuggling in of concepts unjustified by the basic theory is so pervasive and so closely related to behaviorism that another instance or two will serve as an appropriate conclusion to this subsection. Instrumentalism stresses the solving of problems. Dewey emphasizes inquiry: His *Logic* has as a subtitle *The Theory of Inquiry*. "The existence of inquiries is not a matter of doubt. . . . As a mode of conduct, inquiry is as accessible to objective study as are these other modes of behavior" (*Logic, the Theory of Inquiry*, 102). The argument then proceeds upon what Dewey believes the nature of inquiry to be. But, now, what is inquiry? Does not its definition require all the mentalistic terms that behaviorism eschews? On the next page, Dewey repeats for the hundredth time that "dependence upon subjective and 'mentalistic' states and processes is eliminated." It would seem that this allows of only two alternatives. Either mentalistic terms should be rigidly excluded from the discussion, or, if common English words must be used, they should be explicitly defined in non-mentalistic or physical terms. Dewey obviously rejects the first alternative. *Inquiry* itself is mentalistic. *Controlled* inquiry, *directed* experiment, *plans* of action are all mental (*Logic, the Theory of Inquiry*, 104). When Dewey says,

> Organic interaction becomes inquiry when existential consequences are anticipated . . . and when responsive activities are selected and ordered with reference to actualization of some potentialities, rather than others, in a final existential situation" (*Logic, the Theory of Inquiry,* 107),

the words have meaning only in a mentalistic framework. What can anticipation and reference to a future situation mean? These are decidedly subjective and mentalistic terms. Does Dewey anywhere define these common words in non-behavioristic language? No, he does not. For example, there is no explanation of how an unconscious chemical reaction on the retina could anticipate the future or select a plan of action. A physical or physiological event can precede a later event and indeed contribute to its characteristics, just as a precipitate may be formed in a test tube. But this simply is not anticipation, much less selection.

Perhaps Dewey might reply that he had taken care of all this in his theory of language. Environment is cultural, he says, as well as physical. Reactions are ordinarily social:

> This modification of organic behavior in and by the cultural environment accounts for, or rather is, the transformation of purely organic behavior into behavior marked by intellectual properties (*Logic, the Theory of Inquiry,* 43).

Such is Dewey's statement of a transition that behaviorism sorely needs. But in appealing to a culture and a society, Dewey not only assumes that culture could produce his transition in a purely physiological organism, but he also presupposes an unexplained culture and society. Can these be defined behavioristically, or has Dewey substituted two impossibilities for one?

The device on which Dewey chiefly relies to effect this transition is language. Language for Dewey includes not only words but also rites, monuments, tools, and fine art. All these *say* something (*Logic, the Theory of Inquiry,* 46). They operate, he claims, not as mere physical things, but by reason of their meaning. Now, much that Dewey says about the value and use of language is altogether acceptable. The point at issue is how physical motions and effects, tools and words, can take on meaning. If words are supposed to be more than noises emanating from the larynx, they cannot account for the transition that is so necessary to behaviorism, for the transition (if there were any transition) would have already occurred. The intellectual properties must be present in "organisms" before they can assign meaning to noises. Thus Dewey constantly relies on a mind or soul while vigorously denying it.

To this discussion on language he adds a most interesting footnote.

> Generalizing beyond the strict requirements of the position outlined, I would say that I am not aware of any so-called merely "mental" activity or result that cannot be described in the objective terms of an organic activity modified and directed by symbol-meanings, or language, in its broad sense (*Logic, the Theory of Inquiry*, 57).

On Dewey's theory, of course, he could not be *aware* of anything; but on my part, I can interpret this only as a determined refusal to face the problem.

Formal Logic

If behaviorism is untenable, Dewey's genetic, biologically based theory of knowing collapses. We now turn from genetics to the structural aspects of the system. Here the subject is not Logic in its broadest meaning of general epistemology, but the forms of deductive reasoning, the processes of inference, the law of contradiction. To be sure, Dewey does not discuss these matters in much detail. For him, logic as a theory of inquiry is much broader, and his interests are chiefly in that broader part. Nevertheless, what he says, by reason of its generality, includes (as we shall show) a specific view of the principles of deduction. Although Dewey regards this part of logic as of minor importance, the following analysis and criticisms will maintain that it is of major importance and that a tenable view of deductive logic is fatal to the whole of Dewey's philosophy.

In *Logic,* Dewey's very first question is whether the forms of logic have independent subsistence or whether they are forms of subject-matter.

Perhaps it should be immediately noted that Aristotle, to whose logic Dewey objects so strenuously, did not assign his forms an independent subsistence. For Aristotle the forms of logic are secondarily the forms of thought because they are first the forms of being. Logic is based in ontology. What Dewey means by his disjunction will become clear as we proceed. Unfortunately, his initial expression is ambiguous. It may also immediately be noted, in anticipation of many other instances, that Dewey's question covers what we call formal logic (even though it is also ontological) as well as the other phases of inquiry. Indeed he explicitly insists that a theory about the ultimate subject-matter of logic must account for the proximate subject-matter (*Logic, the Theory of Inquiry,* 3), previously identified as relations among propositions, affirmation and negation, inference, and the categorical forms.

What Dewey means by contrasting independently subsistent forms with forms of subject-matter does not long remain in doubt. He proposes that

> all logical forms . . . arise within the operation of inquiry. . . . This conception implies much more than that logical forms are disclosed or come to light when we reflect upon the processes of inquiry that are in use. Of course it means that; but it also means that the forms *originate* in operations of inquiry (*Logic, the Theory of Inquiry,* 3–4).

Specifically mentioning the principles of identity, contradiction, and excluded middle—conclusive evidence that his theory includes these items—Dewey rejects the traditional view that "such principles represent ultimate invariant properties of the *objects* with which methods of inquiry are concerned, and to which inquiry must conform" (*Logic, the Theory of Inquiry,* 11). On the contrary,

> the principles are generated in the very process of control of continued inquiry, while according to the other [traditional] view, there are *a priori* principles fixed antecedently to inquiry and conditioning it *ab extra* (*Logic, the Theory of Inquiry,* 12; compare *Philosophy and Civilization,* 129).

The process by which these principles are generated begins in behavioristic, biological habit. Nothing further will be said about behaviorism, but it is to be noted that if habits change, as they do when unsatisfactory, the new habits will generate new principles. This must be so because a principle or law of logic is simply the formulation of an habitual manner of action. Logic, therefore, improves; it has improved, and it will improve; and this improvement occurs in major matters and not merely in minor details (*Logic, the Theory of Inquiry,* 13–14).

The same theme is stressed on a later page. After asserting that as Greek logic reflected the science of antiquity, so a new logic must be based on modern science, Dewey emphasizes the contrast by quoting and opposing the view of H. W. B. Joseph. Joseph had said,

> It is more in respect of the problems to be answered [by modern science], than of the logical character of the reasoning by which we must prove our answers to them, that Aristotle's view (as represented in the *Topics*) are antiquated.

To this Dewey replies,

> The implication of this passage, especially when it is extended to apply to logical works other than the *Topics,* would seem to be that a radical change in the problems and objects of inquiry (like the change from unchanging substances and their necessary essential forms to correlations of change) can take place with little change in logical forms. . . . A contrary postulate is the

> ground for the present examination of Aristotelian logic (*Logic, the Theory of Inquiry,* 82; compare 156–157, 328–329).

This makes it clear that as scientific interest shifts from one problem to another, there is no part of logic that might not change with it. And if no part of logic escapes change, we must be prepared eventually to abandon the law of contradiction (*Logic, the Theory of Inquiry,* 372, 374 note 2, 391). The same point is borne out by Dewey's comparison of the laws of logic to the laws on contracts (*Logic, the Theory of Inquiry,* 16–17). Comparison with civil law, implying the possibility of change in every part, is found in several places (compare *Logic, the Theory of Inquiry,* 102, 120, 372 ff.).

Further documentation is needless. Dewey holds that no principle of logic is eternal; all are subject to change; great changes have occurred in the past and major improvement is to be expected in the future. The following analysis and criticism consist of two main points. First, an example of alleged improvement will be analyzed and its boast deflated. Second, the impossibility of replacing the law of contradiction will be used to conclude that Dewey's philosophy is basically illogical and irrational.

Existential Import

Following the invention of symbolic logic by George Boole, logicians claimed to find a flaw in Aristotelian subalternation. The introduction of the null class led to the conclusion that the universal implies the particular only when both classes contain existing members. Subalternation therefore is not a general principle because it breaks down in other cases. In contemporary logic textbooks, such as those by Morris Cohen and Ernest Nagel, W. H. Werkmeister, Irving Copi, and indeed nearly all authors, this is expressed for the benefit of elementary students as the existential import of particular propositions. When we say, "All cats are mammals," or, "All snarks are boogums," we do not imply that either cats or snarks exist. But when we say, "Some cats are mammals," and, "Some snarks are boogums," we automatically assert the existence of members of these classes. Therefore A (ab) does not imply I (ab) because the existential import of the latter cannot be deduced from the former.

Now, Dewey uses this as an example of an improvement over and abandonment of Aristotelian logic (*Logic, the Theory of Inquiry,* 255–256, 289–290, 380 and footnote). If, however, this proves not to be the case, a major piece of evidence will drop out of Dewey's position. Dewey himself does not give much argument in favor of existential import. He takes it for granted. Far from implying that this fact reduces criticisms to a carping attack on a trivial detail, the all but universal acceptance of existential import that relieves Dewey of the need to argue it only underscores the importance of this point in non-Aristotelian logic. To meet the argument, therefore, we must turn to other authors. For example, the three textbooks just mentioned, although they omit the symbolic proof, explain the point in ordinary English. But though students have an inordinate reverence for textbooks, anyone who stops to analyze what is being said easily discovers that the alleged conclusion does not follow from the reasons given. For example, Werkmeister, who makes a more determined and fuller attempt than many others to explain existential import, begins by saying that general propositions are to be differentiated from generic propositions.* The latter make no assertion of existence and their terms may be null. The recognition of this distinction is an improvement over Aristotle because not only did Aristotle have no null classes, but, worse, their introduction into Aristotelian logic "leads to discouraging complexities, if not to absurdities" (238).

In a moment, it will be argued that no absurdity arises; even Werkmeister on the next page admits that a general proposition can be translated into a generic proposition. The distinction therefore is useless, and the main defense of existential import must be the following paragraphs.

Unlike generic propositions,

---

*W. H. Werkmeister, *An Introduction to Critical Thinking,* 236–245; 276–277

> particulars cannot be interpreted as being hypothetical in nature. "Some nations desire peace"; this quite obviously does not mean that "if anything is a nation then it desires peace," because such an interpretation would change the proposition into a universal.

This last sentence is quite true. The precise interpretation given has changed the particular into a universal. But this is far from proving that particulars have existential import. If Werkmeister's following sentence is intended to provide the missing proof, it is a failure because it is a mere assertion of the point to be proved.

> The given particular asserts that, *as a matter of fact,* there exist nations which do desire peace. . . . Universal and particular propositions thus differ in their *existential import;* the latter entail an assertion of existence, whereas the former do not (240–241).

Nothing further need be said of arguments in ordinary language. They are usually supported by the addition of diagrams. The universal affirmative, represented by two concentric circles, is supposed to define ab' as null, and $ab=o$ is equated with the negative universal. Not even this is correct, for when the subject or the subject and predicate of the universal affirmative are null, it too exemplifies $ab=o$. Hence Werkmeister is wrong when he says, "the assertion that SP is a null class is the true and complete meaning of the E proposition" (243).

But we are chiefly interested in the particular proposition. Here the author draws two overlapping circles and argues that *ab* or SP do not equal zero. The source of the illusion is the assumption that geometrical areas correctly reproduce all the relations between two classes, and, more pointedly, that they reproduce the relations between null classes. If instead of circles these logicians used points, then perhaps it would be clear that SP is zero when either or both are zero. Therefore the definition of I is not SP = o, and hence there is no existential import.

However, neither arguments in ordinary English nor geometrical diagrams tell the whole story. If one wishes to understand why

Aristotelian subalternation is so uniformly rejected, one must follow through the technical, symbolic proof. Fortunately, this is not too difficult. "All *a* is *b*," or A (ab), is expressed as "class *a* is included in class *b*," or, $a<b$. Now, if A (ab) means $a<b$, then by obversion E (ab) means $a<b'$. By contradicting E, I (ab) becomes $(a<b')'$—the prime signs contradict whatever they are attached to—and O (ab) becomes $(a<b)'$.

Suppose now that A (ab) implies I (ab). In symbols, this is written $(a<b) < (a<b')'$. If this implication is valid, if it holds for every meaning of *a* and *b*, then anything can be substituted for those terms. The term *a* can be null, and the term *b* can also be null. Therefore if Aristotelian subalternation is to be generalized, $(o<o) < (o<o')'$ must be a valid implication. By *valid implication* is meant an inference in which the form of the conclusion is true every time the form of the antecedent is true. Now, the antecedent of this implication, $(o<o)$, is always true. A class is always included in itself. But the conclusion is not true for the following reason. The contradictory of the null class is the universe of discourse. Therefore the conclusion can be rewritten $(o<i)'$. But the universe is the class that contains all classes. If the universe is the human race, it must contain not only men and women, but also the product of these two classes: human beings who are both men and women. This is a null class. Still it is a class because it is the product of classes and therefore is included in the universe. The conclusion being discussed denies that the null class is included in the universe. Therefore the conclusion is false. This makes the implication invalid. Hence a universal, such as, "All cats are mammals," does not validly imply the particular, "Some cats, e.g., Persian cats, are mammals." Such is one of Dewey's chief examples of the breakdown of Aristotelian logic and the modern symbolic improvement.

Lest the reader waste too much time trying to find the loose screw, it should be said that there is no flaw in this process of reasoning. Once the concepts of universe and null are introduced—an improvement to which no Aristotelian need object—and once "All *a* is *b*" is reduced to *a* is included in *b*, the remainder follows automatically. But it does not follow that Aristotelian subalternation breaks down or cannot be generalized. It is quite possible to retain, with the principle of contradiction, the process of obversion by which the definition of E is obtained from A and that of O from I, together with whatever other factors symbolic logic needs, and to retain subalternation also.

It was the late Professor Henry B. Smith* of the University of Pennsylvania who detected the inconclusiveness of the modern argument and worked out symbolically the justification of subalternation. His work deserves more recognition than it has received. Understanding, however, must precede recognition. Smith pointed out that the entire case for non-Aristotelian logic rests upon the choice of a definition. It was assumed that "All *a* is *b*" means "*a* is included in *b*." This assumption is unnecessary. Further, since it leads to the rejection of subalternation, it is also undesirable. At least, if another definition can be framed which will preserve both subalternation and the perfect generality mathematics requires, such a definition will be preferable. Smith formulated such a definition and demonstrated subalternation by it. The formulas at first seems complex, but complexity should not frighten modern symbolic logicians.

$$\begin{aligned} &A\,(ab) = (a<b)\,[(b<a) + (a<b')'(b'<a)'] \\ &E\,(ab) = (a<b')\,[(b'<a) + (a<b)'(b<a)'] \end{aligned}$$

Removing the square brackets, the two lines become:

$$\begin{aligned} &(a<b)(b<a) + (a<b)\,(a<b')'\,(b'<a)' \\ &(a<b')(b'<a) + (a<b')(a<b)'(b<a)' \end{aligned}$$

The product of these two lines is *ipso facto* the product of A E. And if $A\,E = o$, then by contradiction and interchange $A<I$. The multiplication of the two definitions will show that the product is in fact zero.

The product of the six factors following the plus signs contains

**Symbolic Logic*, F. S. Crofts & Co., 1927

$(a<b)(a<b)'$. These two are contradictories and therefore the product is zero.

In each case where the two factors before the plus signs are multiplied into the three factors after the plus sign in the other line, the product contains and therefore is zero.

When the four factors before the plus signs are multiplied, the product reduces to the identification of *b and b'*. The top line identifies *a* and *b;* the second line identifies *a* and *b'*. Therefore a term is identified with its contradictory. This also is a falsity or zero.

Therefore AE implies zero. That is, AE is false. But if so, A implies I, and subalternation is saved.

It is not here claimed that logic cannot in any way be improved. The null class and symbolism generally are improvements. Rather, the claim is that improvements must not discard but must build upon Aristotelian principles. And in particular this subsection shows that the chief non-Aristotelian, or better, anti-Aristotelian improvement is not an improvement at all. The rejection of subalternation leads to a more restricted and less general logic. It is a less fruitful logic because it has fewer valid implications. The Aristotelian scheme is clearly superior.

The Law of Contradiction

Although Dewey does not claim that anyone has discarded the law of contradiction as subalternation has been discarded, his theory implies that future science may very well alter the law of contradiction too. It was seen above that his expressions on the changing nature of logic were all inclusive, and he explicitly mentioned contradiction (*Logic, the Theory of Inquiry,* 11). The reader will remember his criticism of Professor Joseph and how he went on to say that radical changes take place, not only in the details, but in matters of major importance as well.

Beyond this particular documentation it must be noted, both in the immediate contexts of the quotations and in Dewey's voluminous publications as a whole, that universal flux is the warp and woof of his philosophy. Dewey is a philosopher of change and flux. Nothing can be admitted as stable and eternal. To allow even one eternal fixity, the law of contradiction, would in strongest repugnance to his deepest aesthetic nature utterly confuse the fluctuating design of his art. Yet, to contemplate the possibility of a radical change in the law of contradiction is to be already caught in that same confusion.

We have seen that Dewey compares the laws of logic with civil laws. He also speaks of them as stipulations. They are principles of procedure to be adopted and followed so long as they produce satisfactory results. Now, when the interests of science change sufficiently, there may come a time when inquirers will stipulate something radically different from the law of contradiction. What will then occur?

Under the Aristotelian law all clear thinking—past, present, and future—requires a term to have a single significance. Of course, in every language, there are ambiguous words that mean several different things. But so long as these meanings are finite in number, a special term can be assigned to each meaning so that every term would have a single meaning. This is impossible only when a term bears an infinite number of meanings. That is to say, a stipulation radically different from Aristotle's law would require a term, every term, to mean everything. *Zero* would mean both zero and one; *subalternation* would mean both obversion and disjunction. Not only so: *Circle* would mean triangle, ship, southern California, and Columbia University. If the law of contradiction is denied, this result is not merely possible; it is the only possible result. For if we deny that a term can at most mean a finite number of things, we stipulate that it must mean an infinite number of things. Perhaps it will be replied that there is another possibility: The term may mean nothing at all. So be it. The two possibilities are identical, for a term that designates everything designates nothing.

Analyze any sentence whatever. On this stipulation, "Dewey is a philosopher" means "Southern California is a null class," for *Dewey* means California, and *philosopher* is a null class. But these two sentences of identical meaning also signify that Caesar was Socrates and that instrumentalism is nonsense.

The last remark is not a facetious twist to make a humorous point. That instrumentalism is nonsense is the sober and serious result of its theory of logic. The argument in Book Gamma of Aristotle's *Metaphysics* is unanswerable, and it seems significant that the several exponents of contemporary irrationalism neglect its discussion. No implication is here intended that the remainder of Aristotle's writings is flawless. Not only may we discard his physics, but his epistemology with its theory of abstraction may also be untenable. Contrary to Dewey's contention, Aristotle's logic stands alone: As it is not dependent on the state of science in antiquity, so the advances of modern science cannot alter it. Rather it is science that depends on logic. All subjects, all topics of conversation depend on logic, and once the law of contradiction is stipulated away, intelligibility ceases. Therefore instrumentalism is literally nonsense.

Just one further observation is needed to conclude this monograph. The disciple who defends Dewey, if he be now ashamed to predict the repeal of contradiction, may protest that Dewey had not actually discarded it—this was to happen in the future—and that therefore the remainder of instrumentalism is untouched by this criticism.

Probably Dewey would not be overjoyed by his defense. A philosophy of universal flux cannot be happy with any exception. Even one fixed truth would be one too many. Nor is this one truth very easily detached from the remainder of instrumentalism, for if we remove Dewey's principles of logic from his philosophy, what is left falls into unrelated pieces. However, someone in desperation might try to salvage the pieces. Even though they no longer would constitute Dewey's own philosophy, perhaps someone might argue that they could be reconstituted in another form. At any rate, so the contention would go, it is hardly fair to condemn all Dewey has written on the ground that one prediction cannot be fulfilled. The curt answer to this desperate defense is, of course, that Dewey is Dewey; we are not discussing some other philosophy that might emerge in a later reconstruction. But what is more relevant than such a curt reply is that every part of Dewey's position has been examined separately. The arguments against behaviorism relied as little as possible on the fixity of contradiction. Key terms, such as *habit* and *organism,* were analyzed to show their ambiguity. The charge of smuggling was introduced; the covert reductionism was indicated; behaviorism itself, not just formal logic, was attacked. Such also was the procedure with instrumentalism. The discussion dealt with the object of knowledge, the embarrassment of an unknowable existence, ideas as plans of action, and the possibility of history. Then finally with respect to values—a major if not the main subject of interest to Dewey—the criticism, as the subheadings show, was directed from every angle. The argument showed that scientific method cannot justify any preference whatever. Dewey's social and political ideals are in his own system *nothing but* his personal prejudice, and in another system they are judged to be evil. This would be the case even if those ideals were as fixed and eternal as those of Christianity. Only operationalism in the first section of the monograph escaped criticism, and this was because the discussion there tacitly restricted it to physics and chemistry. The operational concept of God, on the contrary, fell under the arguments on instrumentalism.

At the same time and in addition to these points, there is as well the all-pervasive irrationalism of a universal flux that not only denies permanent values but sweeps away even the law of contradiction. The reader is left with a choice, a choice between unintelligibility and fixed principles. If thought has meaning, then there are eternal truths; and while a monograph on Dewey is not the place to expound it, eternal truths require an Eternal Mind whose thinking makes them so.

Bibliography

Brennan, Bernard. *Ethics of William James*. Twayne, 1962.

Buchler, Justus, ed. *Philosophical Writings of Peirce*, 1940.

Dewey, John. *Essays in Experimental Logic*. University of Chicago Press, 1916.

———. *Ethics*. 2d ed. Henry Holt and Company, 1932.

———. *Experience and Nature*. Open Court, 1925.

———. *Human Nature and Conduct*. Henry Holt and Company, 1922.

———. *Logic, the Theory of Inquiry*. Henry Holt and Company, 1938.

———. *Philosophy and Civilization*. Minton, Balch and Company, 1931.

———. *Problems of Men*. Philosophical Library, 1946.

———. *The Quest for Certainty*. Minton, Balch and Company, 1929.

———. *Reconstruction in Philosophy*. Henry Holt and Company, 1920.

Flournoy, Theodore. *The Philosophy of William James*. Holt, 1917.

Gerger, George R. *John Dewey in Perspective*. Oxford University Press, 1958.

Hook, Sidney. *John Dewey: An Intellectual Portrait*, 1939.

James, William. *Essays in Radical Empiricism*, 1912.

———. *A Pluralistic Universe*, 1908.

———. *Pragmatism*, 1907.

Kallen, James, *et al. In Commemoration of William James*. Columbia University Press, 1942.

Kilpatrick, William Heard. *Philosophy of Education*.

Peirce, Charles Sanders. *The Doctrine of Necessity Examined*.

Perry, Ralph Barton. *In the Spirit of William James*. Yale University Press, 1938.

Rolnik, A.A. *William James: His Personality and Contribution*. Science-Art, 1942.

Schilpp, Paul Arthur, ed. *The Philosophy of John Dewey*. Northwestern University, 1939.

Sellery, Otto, *et al. William James, the Man and Thinker*. University of Wisconsin Press, 1942.

Wahl, Jean Andre. *The Pluralist Philosophies of England and America*. Open Court, 1925.
Werkmeister, W.H. *An Introduction to Critical Thinking*.
Williams, Gardner. *Humanistic Ethics*.

Index

The Crisis of Our Time

Historians have christened the thirteenth century the Age of Faith and termed the eighteenth century the Age of Reason. The twentieth century has been called many things: the Atomic Age, the Age of Inflation, the Age of the Tyrant, the Age of Aquarius. But it deserves one name more than the others: the Age of Irrationalism. Contemporary secular intellectuals are anti-intellectual. Contemporary philosophers are anti-philosophy. Contemporary theologians are anti-theology.

In past centuries secular philosophers have generally believed that knowledge is possible to man. Consequently they expended a great deal of thought and effort trying to justify knowledge. In the twentieth century, however, the optimism of the secular philosophers has all but disappeared. They despair of knowledge.

Like their secular counterparts, the great theologians and doctors of the church taught that knowledge is possible to man. Yet the theologians of the twentieth century have repudiated that belief. They also despair of knowledge. This radical skepticism has filtered down from the philosophers and theologians and penetrated our entire culture, from television to music to literature. *The Christian in the twentieth century is confronted with an overwhelming cultural consensus—sometimes stated explicitly, but most often implicitly: Man does not and cannot know anything truly.*

What does this have to do with Christianity? Simply this: If man can know nothing truly, man can truly know nothing. We cannot know that the Bible is the Word of God, that Christ died for the sins of his people, or that Christ is alive today at the right hand of the Father. Unless knowledge is possible, Christianity is nonsensical, for it claims to be knowledge. What is at stake in the twentieth century is not simply a single doctrine, such as the virgin birth, or the existence of Hell, as important as those doctrines may be, but the whole of Christianity itself. If knowledge is not possible to man, it is worse than silly to argue points of doctrine—it is insane.

The irrationalism of the present age is so thoroughgoing and pervasive that even the Remnant—the segment of the professing church that remains faithful—has accepted much of it, frequently without even being aware of what it was accepting. In some circles this irrationalism has become synonymous with piety and humility, and those who oppose it are denounced as rationalists—as though to be logical were a sin. Our contemporary anti-theologians make a contradiction and call it a Mystery. The faithful ask for truth and are given Paradox. If any balk at swallowing the absurdities of the anti-theologians, they are frequently marked as heretics or schismatics who seek to act independently of God.

There is no greater threat facing the true church of Christ at this moment than the irrationalism that now controls our entire culture. Totalitarianism, guilty of tens of millions of murders, including those of millions of Christians, is to be feared, but not nearly so much as the idea that we do not and cannot know the truth. Hedonism, the popular philosophy of America, is not to be feared so much as the belief that logic—that "mere human logic," to use the religious irrationalists' own phrase—is futile. The attacks on truth, on revelation, on the intellect, and on logic are renewed daily. But note well: The misologists—the haters of logic—use logic to demonstrate the futility of using logic. The anti-intellectuals construct intricate intellectual arguments to prove the insufficiency of the intellect. The anti-theologians use the revealed Word of God to show that there can be no revealed Word of God—or that if there could, it would remain impenetrable darkness and Mystery to our finite minds.

Nonsense Has Come

Is it any wonder that the world is grasping at straws—the straws of experientialism, mysticism, and drugs? After all, if people are told that the Bible contains insoluble mysteries, then is not a flight into mysticism to be expected? On what grounds can it be condemned? Certainly not on logical grounds or Biblical grounds, if logic is futile and the Bible unintelligible. Moreover, if it cannot be condemned on logical or Biblical grounds, it cannot be condemned at all. If people are going to have a religion of the mysterious, they will not adopt Christianity: They will have a genuine mystery religion. "Those who call for Nonsense," C.S. Lewis once wrote, "will find that it comes." And that is precisely what has happened. The popularity of Eastern mysticism, of drugs, and of religious experience is the logical consequence of the irrationalism of the twentieth century. There can and will be no new Reformation—and no reconstruction of society—unless and until the irrationalism of the age is totally repudiated by Christians.

The Church Defenseless

Yet how shall they do it? The spokesmen for Christianity have been fatally infected with irrationalism. The seminaries, which annually train thousands of men to teach millions of Christians, are the finishing schools of irrationalism, completing the job begun by the government schools and colleges. Some of the pulpits of the most conservative churches (we are not speaking of the apostate churches) are occupied by graduates of the anti-theological schools. These products of modern anti-theological education, when asked to give a reason for the hope that is in them, can generally respond with only the intellectual analogue of a shrug—a mumble about Mystery. They have not grasped—and therefore cannot teach those for whom they are responsible—the first truth: "And ye shall know the truth." Many, in fact, explicitly deny it, saying that, at best, we possess only "pointers" to the truth, or something "similar" to the truth, a mere analogy. Is the impotence of the Christian church a puzzle? Is the fascination with pentecostalism and faith healing among members of conservative churches an enigma? Not when one understands the sort of studied nonsense that is purveyed in the name of God in the seminaries.

The Trinity Foundation

The creators of The Trinity Foundation firmly believe that theology is too important to be left to the licensed theologians—the graduates of the schools of theology. They have created The Trinity

Foundation for the express purpose of teaching the faithful all that the Scriptures contain—not warmed over, baptized, secular philosophies. Each member of the board of directors of The Trinity Foundation has signed this oath: "I believe that the Bible alone and the Bible in its entirety is the Word of God and, therefore, inerrant in the autographs. I believe that the system of truth presented in the Bible is best summarized in the Westminster Confession of Faith. So help me God."

The ministry of The Trinity Foundation is the presentation of the system of truth taught in Scripture as clearly and as completely as possible. We do not regard obscurity as a virtue, nor confusion as a sign of spirituality. Confusion, like all error, is sin, and teaching that confusion is all that Christians can hope for is doubly sin.

The presentation of the truth of Scripture necessarily involves the rejection of error. The Foundation has exposed and will continue to expose the irrationalism of the twentieth century, whether its current spokesman be an existentialist philosopher or a professed Reformed theologian. We oppose anti-intellectualism, whether it be espoused by a neo-orthodox theologian or a fundamentalist evangelist. We reject misology, whether it be on the lips of a neo-evangelical or those of a Roman Catholic charismatic. To each error we bring the brilliant light of Scripture, proving all things, and holding fast to that which is true.

The Primacy of Theory

The ministry of The Trinity Foundation is not a "practical" ministry. If you are a pastor, we will not enlighten you on how to organize an ecumenical prayer meeting in your community or how to double church attendance in a year. If you are a homemaker, you will have to read elsewhere to find out how to become a total woman. If you are a businessman, we will not tell you how to develop a social conscience. The professing church is drowning in such "practical" advice.

The Trinity Foundation is unapologetically theoretical in its outlook, believing that theory without practice is dead, and that practice without theory is blind. The trouble with the professing church is not primarily in its practice, but in its theory. Christians do not know, and many do not even care to know, the doctrines of Scripture. Doctrine is intellectual, and Christians are generally anti-intellectual. Doctrine is ivory tower philosophy, and they scorn ivory towers. The ivory tower, however, is the control tower of a civilization. It is a fundamental, theoretical mistake of the practical men to think that they can be merely practical, for practice is always the practice of some theory. The relationship between theory and practice is the relationship between cause and effect. If a person believes correct theory, his practice will tend to be correct. The practice of contemporary Christians is immoral because it is the practice of false theories. It is a major theoretical mistake of the practical men to think that they can ignore the ivory towers of the philosophers and theologians as irrelevant to their lives. Every action that the "practical" men take is governed by the thinking that has occurred in some ivory tower—whether that tower be the British Museum, the Academy, a home in Basel, Switzerland, or a tent in Israel.

In Understanding Be Men

It is the first duty of the Christian to understand correct theory—correct doctrine—and thereby implement correct practice. This order—first theory, then practice—is both logical and Biblical. It is, for example, exhibited in Paul's epistle to the Romans, in which he spends the first eleven chapters expounding theory and the last five discussing practice. The contemporary teachers of Christians have not only reversed the order, they have inverted the Pauline emphasis on theory and practice. The virtually complete failure of the teachers of the professing church to instruct the faithful in correct doctrine is the cause of the misconduct and cultural impotence of Christians. The church's lack of power is the result of its lack of truth. The *Gospel* is the power of God, not religious experience or personal relationship. The church has no power because it has abandoned the Gospel, the good news, for a religion of experientialism. Twentieth-century American Christians are children carried about by every wind of doctrine, not knowing what they believe, or even if they believe anything for certain.

The chief purpose of The Trinity Foundation is to counteract the irrationalism of the age and to expose the errors of the teachers of the church. Our emphasis—on the Bible as the sole source of truth, on the primacy of the intellect, on the supreme importance of correct doctrine, and on the necessity for systematic and logical thinking—is almost unique in Christendom. To the extent that the church survives—and she will survive and flourish—it will be because of her increasing acceptance of these basic ideas and their logical implications.

We believe that The Trinity Foundation is filling a vacuum in Christendom. We are saying that Christianity is intellectually defensible—that, in fact, it is the only intellectually defensible system of thought. We are saying that God has made the wisdom of this world—whether that wisdom be called science, religion, philosophy, or common sense—foolishness. We are appealing to all Christians who have not conceded defeat in the intellectual battle with the world to join us in our efforts to raise a standard to which all men of sound mind can repair.

The love of truth, of God's Word, has all but disappeared in our time. We are committed to and pray for a great instauration. But though we may not see this reformation of Christendom in our lifetimes, we believe it is our duty to present the whole counsel of God because Christ has commanded it. The results of our teaching are in God's hands, not ours. Whatever those results, his Word is never taught in vain, but always accomplishes the result that he intended it to accomplish. Professor Gordon H. Clark has stated our view well:

> There have been times in the history of God's people, for example, in the days of Jeremiah, when refreshing grace and widespread revival were not to be expected: The time was one of chastisement. If this twentieth century is of a similar nature, individual Christians here and there can find comfort and strength

> in a study of God's Word. But if God has decreed happier days for us and if we may expect a world-shaking and genuine spiritual awakening, then it is the author's belief that a zeal for souls, however necessary, is not the sufficient condition. Have there not been devout saints in every age, numerous enough to carry on a revival? Twelve such persons are plenty. What distinguishes the arid ages from the period of the Reformation, when nations were moved as they had not been since Paul preached in Ephesus, Corinth, and Rome, is the latter's fullness of knowledge of God's Word. To echo an early Reformation thought, when the ploughman and the garage attendant know the Bible as well as the theologian does, and know it better than some contemporary theologians, then the desired awakening shall have already occurred.

In addition to publishing books, the Foundation publishes a monthly newsletter, *The Trinity Review*. Subscriptions to *The Review* are free; please write to the address below to become a subscriber. If you would like further information or would like to join us in our work, please let us know.

The Trinity Foundation is a non-profit foundation tax-exempt under section 501(c)(3) of the Internal Revenue Code of 1954. You can help us disseminate the Word of God through your tax-deductible contributions to the Foundation.

And we know that the Son of God has come, and has given us an understanding, that we may know him that is true, and we are in him that is true, in his Son Jesus Christ. This is the true God, and eternal life.

John W. Robbins

Intellectual Ammunition

The Trinity Foundation is committed to the reconstruction of philosophy and theology along Biblical lines. We regard God's command to bring all our thoughts into conformity with Christ very seriously, and the books listed below are designed to accomplish that goal. They are written with two subordinate purposes: (1) to demolish all secular claims to knowledge; and (2) to build a system of truth based upon the Bible alone.

Philosophy

Behaviorism and Christianity, Gordon H. Clark $6.95

Behaviorism *is a critique of both secular and religious behaviorists. It includes chapters on John Watson, Edgar S. Singer Jr., Gilbert Ryle, B.F. Skinner, and Donald MacKay. Clark's refutation of behaviorism and his argument for a Christian doctrine of man are unanswerable.*

A Christian Philosophy of Education $8.95
Gordon H. Clark

The first edition of this book was published in 1946. It sparked the contemporary interest in Christian schools. Dr. Clark thoroughly revised and updated it, and it is needed now more than ever. Its chapters include: The Need for a World-View, The Christian World-View, The Alternative to Christian Theism, Neutrality, Ethics, The Christian Philosophy of Education, Academic Matters, Kindergarten to University. Three appendices are included as well: The Relationship of Public Education to Christianity, A Protestant World-View, and Art and the Gospel.

A Christian View of Men and Things $10.95
Gordon H. Clark

No other book achieves what A Christian View *does: the pre-*

sentation of Christianity as it applies to history, politics, ethics, science, religion, and epistemology. Clark's command of both worldly philosophy and Scripture is evident on every page, and the result is a breathtaking and invigorating challenge to the wisdom of this world.

Clark Speaks From The Grave, Gordon H. Clark $3.95

Dr. Clark chides some of his critics for their failure to defend Christianity competently. Clark Speaks *is a stimulating and illuminating discussion of the errors of contemporary apologists.*

Education, Christianity, and the State $8.95
J. Gresham Machen

Machen was one of the foremost educators, theologians, and defenders of Christianity in the twentieth century. The author of numerous scholarly books, Machen saw clearly that if Christianity is to survive and flourish, a system of Christian grade schools must be established. This collection of essays captures his thoughts on education over nearly three decades.

Essays on Ethics and Politics, Gordon H. Clark $10.95

Clark's essays, written over the course of five decades, are a major statement of Christian ethics.

Gordon H. Clark: Personal Recollections $6.95
John W. Robbins, editor

Friends of Dr. Clark have written their recollections of the man. Contributors include family members, colleagues, students, and friends such as Harold Lindsell, Carl Henry, Ronald Nash, Dwight Zeller, and Mary Crumpacker. The book includes an extensive bibliography of Clark's work.

Historiography: Secular and Religious $13.95
Gordon H. Clark

In this masterful work, Clark applies his philosophy to the writing of history, examining all the major schools of historiography.

An Introduction to Christian Philosophy $8.95
Gordon H. Clark

In 1966 Clark delivered three lectures on philosophy at Wheaton College. In these lectures he criticizes secular philosophy and launches a philosophical revolution in the name of Christ.

Language and Theology, Gordon H. Clark $9.95

There are two main currents in twentieth-century philosophy—language philosophy and existentialism. Both are hostile to Christianity. Clark disposes of language philosophy in this brilliant critique of Bertrand Russell, Ludwig Wittgenstein, Rudolf Carnap, A.J. Ayer, Langdon Gilkey, and many others.

Logic, Gordon H. Clark $8.95

Written as a textbook for Christian schools, Logic *is another unique book from Clark's pen. His presentation of the laws of thought, which must be followed if Scripture is to be understood correctly, and which are found in Scripture itself, is both clear and thorough.* Logic *is an indispensable book for the thinking Christian.*

Logic Workbook, Elihu Carranza $11.95

Designed to be used in conjunction with Clark's textbook Logic, *this* Workbook *contains hundreds of exercises and test questions on perforated pages for ease of use by students.*

Logic Workbook Answer Key, Elihu Carranza $4.95

The Key *contains answers to all the exercises and tests in the* Workbook.

Lord God of Truth, Concerning the Teacher $7.95
Gordon H. Clark and Aurelius Augustine

This essay by Clark summarizes many of the most telling arguments against empiricism and defends the Biblical teaching that we know God and truth immediately. The dialogue by Augustine is a refutation of empirical language philosophy.

The Philosophy of Science and Belief in God $7.95
Gordon H. Clark

In opposing the contemporary idolatry of science, Clark analyzes three major aspects of science: the problem of motion, Newtonian science, and modern theories of physics. His conclusion is that science, while it may be useful, is always false; and he demonstrates its falsity in numerous ways. Since science is always false, it can offer no objection to the Bible and Christianity.

Religion, Reason and Revelation, Gordon H. Clark $9.95

One of Clark's apologetical masterpieces, Religion, Reason and Revelation *has been praised for the clarity of its thought and language. It includes chapters on Is Christianity a Religion?, Faith and Reason, Inspiration and Language, Revelation and Morality, and God and Evil. It is must reading for all serious Christians.*

Thales to Dewey: A History of Philosophy paper $11.95
Gordon H. Clark hardback $16.95

This is the best one-volume history of philosophy in English.

Three Types of Religious Philosophy $6.95
Gordon H. Clark

In this book on apologetics, Clark examines empiricism, rationalism, dogmatism, and contemporary irrationalism, which does not rise to the level of philosophy. He offers a solution to the question, "How can Christianity be defended before the world?"

William James and John Dewey $8.95
Gordon H. Clark

William James and John Dewey are two of the most influential philosophers America has produced. Their philosophies of instrumentalism and pragmatism are hostile to Christianity, and Clark demolishes their arguments completely.

Theology

The Atonement, Gordon H. Clark $8.95

This is a major section of Clark's multi-volume systematic theology. In The Atonement, *Clark discusses the covenants, the virgin birth and incarnation, federal headship and representation, the relationship between God's sovereignty and justice, and much more. He analyzes traditional views of the atonement and criticizes them in the light of Scripture alone.*

The Biblical Doctrine of Man, Gordon H. Clark $6.95

Is man soul and body or soul, spirit, and body? What is the image of God? Is Adam's sin imputed to his children? Is evolution true? Are men totally depraved? What is the heart? These are some of the questions discussed and answered from Scripture in this book.

Cornelius Van Til: The Man and The Myth $2.45
John W. Robbins

The actual teachings of this eminent Philadelphia theologian have been obscured by the myths that surround him. This book penetrates those myths and criticizes Van Til's surprisingly unorthodox views of God and the Bible.

The Everlasting Righteousness, Horatius Bonar $8.95

Originally published in 1874, the language of Bonar's masterpiece on justification by faith alone has been updated and Americanized for easy reading and clear understanding. This is one of the best books ever written on justification.

Faith and Saving Faith, Gordon H. Clark $6.95

The views of the Roman Catholic church, John Calvin, Thomas Manton, John Owen, Charles Hodge, and B.B. Warfield are discussed in this book. Is the object of faith a person or a proposition? Is faith more than belief? Is belief more than thinking with assent, as Augustine said? In a world chaotic with differing views of faith, Clark clearly explains the Biblical view of faith and saving faith.

God's Hammer: The Bible and Its Critics $8.95
Gordon H. Clark

The starting point of Christianity, the doctrine on which all other doctrines depend, is "The Bible alone is the Word of God written, and therefore inerrant in the autographs." Over the centuries the opponents of Christianity, with Satanic shrewdness, have concentrated their attacks on the truthfulness and completeness of the Bible. In the twentieth century the attack is not so much in the fields of history and archaeology as in philosophy. Clark's brilliant defense of the complete truthfulness of the Bible is captured in this collection of eleven major essays.

Guide to the Westminster Confession and Catechism $13.95
James E. Bordwine

This large book contains the full text of both the Westminster Confession (both original and American versions) and the Larger Catechism. In addition, it offers a chapter-by-chapter summary of the Confession and a unique index to both the Confession and the Catechism.

The Holy Spirit, Gordon H. Clark $8.95

This discussion of the third person of the Trinity is both concise and exact. Clark includes chapters on the work of the Spirit, santification, and Pentecostalism. This book is part of his multi-volume systematic theology that began appearing in print in 1985.

The Incarnation, Gordon H. Clark $8.95

Who is Christ? The attack on the incarnation in the nineteenth and twentieth centuries has been vigorous, but the orthodox response has been lame. Clark reconstructs the doctrine of the incarnation, building and improving upon the Chalcedonian definition.

In Defense of Theology, Gordon H. Clark $9.95

There are four groups to whom Clark addresses this book: average Christians who are uninterested in theology, atheists and agnostics, religious experientialists, and serious Christians. The vindication of the knowledge of God against the objections of three of these groups is the first step in theology.

The Johannine Logos, Gordon H. Clark $5.95

Clark analyzes the relationship between Christ, who is the truth, and the Bible. He explains why John used the same word to refer to both Christ and his teaching. Chapters deal with the Prologue to John's Gospel, Logos and Rheemata, Truth, and Saving Faith.

Justification by Faith Alone, Charles Hodge $8.95

Charles Hodge of Princeton Seminary was the best American theologian of the nineteenth century. Here in one volume are his two major essays on justification. This book is essential in defending the faith.

Predestination, Gordon H. Clark $8.95

Clark thoroughly discusses one of the most controversial and pervasive doctrines of the Bible: that God is, quite literally, Almighty. Free will, the origin of evil, God's omniscience, creation, and the new birth are all presented within a Scriptural framework. The objections of those who do not believe in the Almighty God are considered and refuted. This edition also contains the text of the booklet, Predestination in the Old Testament.

Sanctification, Gordon H. Clark $8.95

In this book, which is part of Clark's multi-volume systematic theology, he discusses historical theories of sanctification, the sacraments, and the Biblical doctrine of sanctification.

Scripture Twisting in the Seminaries
Part 1: Feminism, John W. Robbins $5.95

An analysis of the views of three graduates of Westminster Seminary on the role of women in the church.

Today's Evangelism: Counterfeit or Genuine? $6.95
Gordon H. Clark

Clark compares the methods and messages of today's evangelists with Scripture, and finds that Christianity is on the wane because the Gospel has been distorted or lost. This is an extremely useful and enlightening book.

The Trinity, Gordon H. Clark $8.95

Apart from the doctrine of Scripture, no teaching of the Bible is more important than the doctrine of God. Clark's defense of the orthodox doctrine of the Trinity is a principal portion of Clark's systematic theology. There are chapters on the deity of Christ, Augustine, the incomprehensibility of God, Bavinck and Van Til, and the Holy Spirit, among others.

What Calvin Says, W. Gary Crampton $7.95

This is both a readable and thorough introduction to the theology of John Calvin.

What Do Presbyterians Believe? Gordon H. Clark $8.95

This classic introduction to Christian doctrine has been republished. It is the best commentary on the Westminster Confession of Faith that has ever been written.

Commentaries on the New Testament

Colossians, Gordon H. Clark $6.95
Ephesians, Gordon H. Clark $8.95
First Corinthians, Gordon H. Clark $10.95
First John, Gordon H. Clark $10.95
First and Second Thessalonians, Gordon H. Clark $5.95
New Heavens, New Earth (First and Second Peter) $10.95
Gordon H. Clark
The Pastoral Epistles (I and II Timothy and Titus) $9.95
Gordon H. Clark

All of Clark's commentaries are expository, not technical, and are written for the Christian layman. His purpose is to explain the text clearly and accurately so that the Word of God will be thoroughly known by every Christian.

The Trinity Library

We will send you one copy of each of the 45 books listed above for $250. You may also order the books you want individually on the order blank on the next page. Because some of the books are in short supply, we must reserve the right to substitute others of equal or greater value in The Trinity Library. This special offer expires June 30, 1997.

ORDER FORM

Name ____

Address ____

____

Please: ☐ add my name to the mailing list for *The Trinity Review*. I understand that there is no charge for the *Review* in the United States. (Ten dollars per year to foreign addresses.)

☐ accept my tax deductible contribution of $________ for the work of the Foundation.

☐ send me __________ copies of *William James and John Dewey*. I enclose as payment $____________.

☐ send me the Trinity Library of 45 books. I enclose $250 as full payment.

☐ send me the following books. I enclose full payment in the amount of $__________ for them.

____

____

____

____

____

____

Mail to:

The Trinity Foundation
Post Office Box 1666
Hobbs, NM 88240